Post-Industrial AMERICA

DAVID CLARK

Post-Industrial
AMERICA

A geographical perspective

METHUEN
New York and London

First published in 1984 by Methuen, Inc.
733 Third Avenue, New York, NY 10017
Published in Great Britain by Methuen & Co. Ltd
11 New Fetter Lane, London EC4P 4EE

Typeset in Hong Kong by Graphicraft Typesetters
and printed in Great Britain at the
University Press, Cambridge

Library of Congress Cataloging in Publication Data
Clark, David, Ph. D.
    Post-industrial America.

    Bibliography: p.
    Includes index.
    1. United States—Economic conditions—1945–
I. Title.
HC106.5.C5826   1985   330.973'092   84-14851
ISBN 0-416-38250-9
ISBN 0-416-38260-6 (pbk.)

British Library Cataloguing in Publication Data
Clark, David, 19-
    Post industrial America.
    1. Anthropo-geography—United States
    2. United States—Social conditions—1980–
    I. Title.
    303.4'0973   GF503

    ISBN 0-416-38250-9
    ISBN 0-416-38260-6 Pbk

For Judith and Hannah Lucy

Contents

Preface

In 1950, the population of the United States, at 150 million, was growing rapidly. Seven out of every ten Americans lived in cities, the majority in central areas, and a continuing expansion of megalopolis and the largest metropolises seemed inevitable. Conversely, non-metropolitan localities were in general characterized by out-migration and economic decline. Thirty per cent of the workforce was employed in manufacturing industry which, because of cheap energy and technological and product leadership, enjoyed an unchallenged superiority in domestic and many international markets. As a consequence, the major manufacturing regions of the North-East and Mid-West were strong and successful, whereas the South and West, with their predominantly resource-based and non-manufacturing economies, lagged behind in terms of levels of economic development and material prosperity. Aid, in the form of increased expenditure on public works, tax incentives, and subsidies, was available to enable backward areas to reach parity with other regions.

Today, a very different set of patterns and trends is apparent. Although the population has risen to 220 million, a dramatic decline in birth rates has reduced population growth to replacement levels. Net rural out-migration has ceased, and the largest cities, and especially their central areas, are experiencing major population and employment loss. Manufacturing is no longer the source of employment growth, and the emphasis is upon the quaternary and the quinary sectors. Resource-based territories are stronger and energy supply problems dominate in determining the relative advantages of different regions. The sunbelt is progressively overshadowing the frostbelt. The North-East and Mid-West rather than the South and West are lagging regions while the latter are areas of population growth and economic expansion.

In identifying some of the more pronounced contrasts between mid-century and contemporary America, the cameos presented in the last two paragraphs underline the nature and magnitude of post-war change. They highlight the major geographical conse-quences of the complex set of transformations that are associated as part causes and part effects of the country's progression from an advanced industrial to a post-industrial economy and society. Such structural alterations involve deep-seated shifts of social, econo-mic, and technological order that amount to the emergence of a new and different social formation over the past forty years. In turn, this has had, and is having, a profound impact upon the arrange-ment and distribution of population, industry, agriculture, cities, and regions. The locational corollaries of structural change form the focus of this book. Specifically, it outlines and evaluates the emerging geography of post-industrial America.

As a survey of a defined area of territory, this text is essentially a work in "regional geography." It outlines, summarizes and attempts to account for the contemporary distribution of economic and social activities, and the ways in which they overlap and interdigi-tate to form areas of specialization within the country. In place of a traditional regional format with individual sections on physical structure, relief, climate, soils, population, industries, and cities, however, this text has an essentially thematic arrangement. Its organization and content follow from the underlying thesis that the contemporary and changing geography of the United States is a product of the evolving structure of the society and the economy. Chapter 1 provides the general background by outlining and evaluating the salient characteristics of industrial and post-industrial America, and the geographical causes and consequences are discussed in the five succeeding chapters. These focus in turn upon the current and changing distribution of population, of industry and employment, and of agricultural production, and upon trends and problems at the urban and regional scales. A comparison of patterns and trends between 1950 and 1980 is the basic methodology used in the five substantive chapters, the presentation and discussion of tables from the most recent 1980 census being a particular focus where appropriate.

Many individuals in widely scattered locations have contributed, both consciously and inadvertently, to the content and orientation of this book. I am especially grateful to Neil Salisbury and members of staff in the Department of Geography, University of Oklahoma, where I spent a most profitable sabbatical term in 1981, gaining first-hand experience of current trends in the geography of the United States. Thanks are also due to David Smith and colleagues in the Department of Geography, Coventry (Lanchester) Polytechnic, for facilitating and covering for my absence.

Detailed and most helpful comments on Chapter 5 were provided by Brian Ilbery, and maps and diagrams were expertly drawn by Mary Merrell. To both I am heavily indebted. Despite persistent attempts over the years to increase its popularity, the "Geography of the United States" remains a cinderella course within the Modern Studies degree program in Coventry Polytechnic. If this book persuades only a handful of students that the contemporary processes of socio-economic and spatial change in America are worthy of detailed investigation, then at least one of its aims will have been achieved.

David Clark

Coventry

1984

List of figures

List of tables

1

Industrial and post-industrial America

The United States has a history of rapidly changing economic and associated geographical development. Before independence, trading links were primarily with Europe so eastern seaports rose to prominence as centers of colonial economy and society. Agricultural and production specialisms among their hinterlands varied considerably because of environmental and historical circumstances, so that basic differences of social and spatial order characterized the northern, mid-Atlantic, and southern states. With the frontier phase in the mid-nineteenth century, a network of new communities, interconnected by the railroad, sprang up to service the needs of the agricultural interior. Distributed according to central place principles, settlements varied in size from hamlet to market town, and social and economic life correspondingly reflected position along the rural–urban gradient. Later, new production technologies created an urban–industrial economy in the North-East and along the Lake Shore. This formed the central focus of a network of regions across the nation within which economic and social activities were determined by distance from, and accessibility to, the manufacturing heartland. Fundamental contrasts of locational arrangement and spatial organization characterized these different developmental eras. A distinctive geography is associated with each formative stage in the historical evolution of modern America.

These different geographical relationships were essentially products of territory and society. Each represented a spatial arrangement of people and activities designed to suit the requirements of the prevailing economic and social patterns. The distribution of population, the siting of industry, patterns of agricultural and regional specialization, and the size, spacing, and functions of cities all reflected the operation of allocative, locational, and organizational principles within society and the economy. For example, during the pre-independence era, the southern colonies were developed to provide the raw materials of cotton, indigo, sugar, and tobacco required by Western Europe. Agriculture was organized on the basis of large estates, and the products were shipped direct, without undergoing secondary processing, from tidewater locations. As a result, the social system was essentially two-tier, consisting of aristocratic landowners and subservient field workers. Southern society and economy in turn imposed their imprints upon the landscape which was structured around the plantation as the primary unit of spatial organization (Thistlethwaite, 1961). In contrast, the northern colonies had a far greater degree of autonomy, self-reliance, and freedom of action, by virtue of their puritan origins. The need to pursue the goals of self-sufficiency and economic separation gave rise to an urban middle class of craftsmen, merchants, and artisans who progressively made the colonies self-sufficient. In consequence, New England evolved as an urban-agricultural economy within which the town was the essential social and spatial pivot. But just as societal structure in the southern and nothern colonies determined a spatial response, so economic and social development triggered a set of geographical adjustments. The geography of the colonial period was replaced by equally distinctive and symbiotic geographies of the frontier and, subsequently, of the urban-industrial eras. The history of American development shows that no sooner were people and jobs arranged and positioned in accordance with societal demand, than the emergence of a succeeding social and economic order stimulated movement, migration, and relocation, culminating in the emergence of a new geography.

The importance of the link between social form and geographical pattern is emphasized most strongly in structuralist theory. The basic thesis of the structuralist approach is that an explanation of spatial patterns is impossible from the study of the patterns themselves. Geographical distributions are brought about by processes that are an integral part of the operation of the economy and society; indeed, they reflect and help to maintain those processes. Instead of trying to infer the nature of the underlying causal processes from the geographical patterns which they create, it is essential to analyse the processes themselves. These processes, in turn, are a product of the infrastructural relationships within society which give society its form and character. They include the nature of the economy, the social structure, levels and use of technology, bases and distribution of power, and the role of institutions. Together, these parameters define the social formation, composed of economic, political, and ideological values which combine and function as a complex whole. The social formation in turn is both dependent upon and gives rise to a particular spatial arrangement of society and the economy. Social structure and geography are interdependent in that the spatial organization of a particular state both reflects and helps to sustain the prevailing social formation.

The closeness of this link means that as social and economic development proceeds, so the social formation changes and, in consequence, new and different geographical patterns and distributions are created. Just as the geography of pre-industrial America was a product of mercantilism and colonialism, and that of mid-twentieth century America was a response to the needs of industrialism, so the geography of America in the 1980s has its explanations deep in the contemporary social formation. Its origins lie in present-day social, economic, and political institutions, structures, values, and preferences. This chapter provides a general background to the understanding of the geography of modern America by examining the emerging social formation. Specifically it outlines and evaluates the salient characteristics of mid-century industrial, and contemporary post-industrial, America.

Industrial America

The United States evolved from a pre-industrial to a post-industrial economy and society in little more than a century. This development involved a sequence of profound social and economic changes which in turn transformed and are transforming the geography of the nation. Precise timings and terminology vary among analysts but there is general agreement on the major turning points in the course of American economic development. For Rostow (1965) there were five stages. Each is identified in terms of the characteristics of investment, production, and consumption. The build-up to, and characteristics of, the fifth stage is of greatest relevance here as it defines one element in the economic backcloth to twentieth century America.

Until 1840, the United States was, in Rostow's terms, a traditional society. The overriding characteristic was a generally low level of development of science and technology which imposed an effective ceiling upon the level of attainable output per head. As a consequence, a high proportion of resources was devoted to food production, and, following from the needs of agriculture, there was a rigid hierarchical social system. A transformation of this traditional society was made possible in the 1840s when the pre-requisites for rapid economic growth based upon industry were established. Of central importance was a radical shift in attitudes towards fundamental and applied science, the introduction of changes in productive technology, towards risk-taking and towards work. The increased commitment to economic progress was most clearly seen in the increase in the rate of investment to a level which regularly, substantially, and perceptibly, outstripped population growth. This in turn resulted in the build-up of social overhead capital, especially in the railroads, which provided the springboard for a succeeding phase of rapid economic growth.

A major watershed in economic development occurred in the third stage, the take-off. This was the period when the old blocks and resistances to economic development were finally overcome, and rapid and compound economic growth became the normal condition. During the take-off, the rate of effective investment and savings rose to 10 per cent or more of national income and was concentrated in a small number of leading sectors where growth performance provided the catalyst for more general economic change. For Rostow, the American take-off occurred between 1843 and 1860 and was distinguished by two phases. The first, in the 1840s, marked by railway and manufacturing development, was mainly confined to the East. It occurred while the West and South digested the extensive agricultural expansion of the previous decade. The second was the great railroad push into the Mid-West during the 1850s. By the opening of the Civil War in 1861, the foundations of industrial America are judged to have been established.

After take-off there followed a long interval of sustained if fluctuating progress as the expanding economy extended industrial technology over a wide front. During the drive to maturity, the economy demonstrated a capacity to move beyond the original industries which powered its take-off, and to apply contemporary technology to an extensive range of industrial processes and activities. What was involved was a shift in focus from the coal, iron, and heavy engineering industries of the railroad phase to machine tools, chemicals, and electrical equipment. Indicative of this change was the replacement by 1920 of agriculture by manufacturing as the major employment sector in the economy (Figure 1.1). This national trend, however, concealed important regional variations in that the South and West lagged considerably behind the North-East in terms of general level of industrial development.

The final transformation associated with the rise of industrial America was the achievement of high mass-consumption. What distinguished this from preceding phases was a fundamental shift in emphasis from supply to demand, from problems of production to problems of consumption and welfare in the widest sense. As real incomes rose to levels well in excess of those necessary to secure basic food, shelter, and clothing, so demand was generated for a wide range of consumer goods and services. In consequence, the economic base was extended to include the manufacture of bicycles, cars, aircraft, household appliances, and luxury goods. These in turn increased the level of activity in housing and general construction, in public utility provision, and in transportation. The turning point was perhaps Henry Ford's moving assembly line of 1913–14 which demonstrated the feasibility of mass production of consumer goods, but it was in the 1920s and again in the 1940s that this stage of demand-led growth was pursued to its logical conclusion. Prosperity was also reflected in the birth rate which, though fluctuating, remained in excess of 24 per 1000 over the period 1920–60. This, combined with a declining death rate (and migration rate), resulted in the addition of 73 million people to the population between 1920 and 1960.

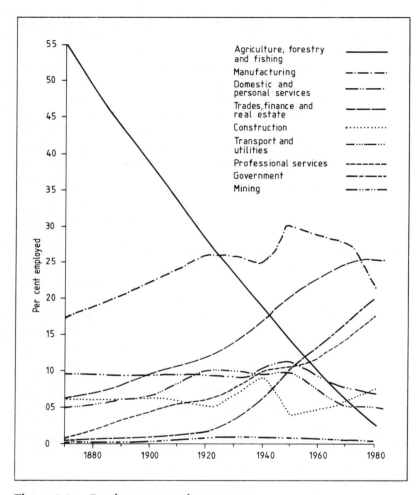

Figure 1.1 *Employment trends, 1870–1980*

Despite this population growth, the mass-consumption economy proved more than able to satisfy the increasingly varied and complex needs of the industrial society. By 1956, 73 per cent of families owned their own cars, 96 per cent of houses wired for electricity had refrigerators, and 86 per cent televisions. The effect of this increased demand was to further emphasize the importance of industrial production, so that at its peak in 1950 the manufacturing sector accounted for 30 per cent of the labor force (Figure 1.1). Industrial expansion was similarly reflected in the level of trade, financial, and real estate activity, which was responsible for 20 per cent of employment, and by the growth in the number of jobs in transportation and utilities, and professional services. Each accounted in 1950 for 8 per cent of the labor force. Increased national wealth enabled greater resources to be devoted to welfare programs and to defense. The task of managing industrial production increased the proportion of the population working in offices or in skilled factory jobs, and living in towns and cities. The manufacturing plant, the office, and the industrial metropolis were indeed the most powerful visual symbols of high mass-consumption industrial America.

Important though these economic developments were, they were only one facet of a wider set of structural characteristics that were indicative of the rise of industrialism. As the economic structure changed, values, expectations, and lifestyles changed with it so that America was transformed by the first quarter of the twentieth century into an industrial society. For Bell (1973), society consists of three parts; the social structure, the polity, and the culture. The social structure comprises the economy and technology. The polity regulates the distribution of power and adjudicates the conflicting claims and demands of individuals and groups. The culture is the realm of expressive symbolism and meaning. On these bases it is possible to distinguish industrial society from the post-industrial forms which succeeded it (Table 1.1).

The essence of industrial society was its emphasis upon goods production. The overall "design" was indeed a "game against fabricated nature," centered upon man–machine relationships, which involved the use of energy to transform the natural environment into a technical environment. Manufacturing was the key economic sector, the needs of industry affecting every aspect of social life. In particular, they determined the distribution of power and wealth, the structure of the labor force, the pattern of daily routine, and the orientation of education and research. Industrial strength was based upon energy from coal and oil, and the central problem of industrial society was that of maximizing profits by minimizing the costs of the basic factors of production, including land, labor, and capital, and sustaining the highest output possible of manufactured goods. Economic growth was regarded as the

Table 1.1   *Structural characteristics of industrial and post-industrial society*

Characteristic social structure	Industrial	Post-industrial
Design	Game against fabricated nature	Game between persons
Economic sector	*Secondary* Processing Manufacturing	*Tertiary* Transportation Utilities *Quaternary* Trade Finance Insurance Real Estate *Quinary* Health Education Research Government Recreation Information
Technology	Energy	
Axial principle	Economic growth: State or private control of investment decisions	Centrality and codification of theoretical knowledge
Occupational slope	Semi-skilled worker Engineer	Professional and technical scientists
Time perspective	Ad hoc adaptiveness	Future orientation Forecasting
Polity		
Resource	Machinery	Knowledge
Social focus	Business firm	University Research Institute
Dominant figures	Businessmen	Scientists Researchers
Means of power	Indirect influence on politics	Balance of technical-political forces Franchises and rights
Class base	Property Political organization Technical skill	Technical skill Political organization
Access	Inheritance Patronage Education	Education Mobilization Co-option

Source: Bell (1973).

overriding national objective and occasioned intervention in the economy by government so as to create the optimum environment for industry. Turnover was maintained at a high level by advertising designed to create demand for the many and varied products of the industrial economy, as Galbraith (1958) has observed. Frequent model changes and built-in obsolescence helped further to inflate consumption but at the expense of the wasteful use of finite resources (Packard, 1961).

Industrial America had a distinctive employment structure. With mass-production techniques and the universal use of machinery, labor was highly specialized, and the engineer, responsible for the layout and flow of work, and the semi-skilled worker, the human cog between machines, were key personnel. Technical competence rather than craft ability was the most important qualification for employment in industry. Servicing the needs of industry and, in particular, co-ordinating men, material, and markets, involved work in transportation, public utilities, wholesale and retail distribution, finance, real estate, and insurance. Domination of production by the industrial corporation meant that the businessman, rather than the farmer or the military officer, monopolized power in industrial society. The focus of social relations was the enterprise or firm. Access to power was by inheritance, patronage, or through educa-tion. Class and status divisions were relatively rigid and depended to a large extent upon type and level of work. The major social problems arose from conflicts between employer and worker.

The success of industry depended upon its capacity to innovate and to introduce new processes and products. The link between science and technology was, however, tenuous and indirect. Bell argues that the major industries of the high mass-consumption economy—steel, telegraph, telephone, electricity, automobile, and aviation—were essentially nineteenth century industries in that they were mainly the creation of inventors, inspired or talented tinkerers, who were indifferent to science and the fundamental laws underlying their investigations. Technological progress was largely the result of inspired *ad hoc* experimentation. For example, Edison's work on electric sparks, which led to the development of the electric light and generated a vast new revolution in technology, was undertaken outside the theoretical research in electromagnet-ism and even in hostility to it. Similarly, Alexander Graham Bell, inventor of the telephone, was, according to Clerk Maxwell, "a mere elocutionist turned electrician." Technological progress was essentially achieved through trial and error; the contribution made by theoretical science was minimal.

With the predominance of the machine, the rhythm of life in industrial society was mechanically paced. Time was a precious commodity, and, with the need to synchronize movements of raw materials and finished products so as to maintain the flow of goods, the success of industry depended upon scheduling and programming. The lengths of shifts and the spacing of holidays divided the days and the year into work, leisure, and recreation periods. Bell's generalizations are of course idealized, but taken together they summarize the salient characteristics of the industrial society which existed in the United States between the second and fifth decades of the twentieth century.

The geography of industrial America

What were the geographical corollaries of the high mass-consumption industrial society? This question was addressed by several generations of research workers in the inter-war and immediate post-war periods from the standpoints of their individual systematic specialisms. Foremost among the contributions in demography were the studies by Bogue (1959) and Taeuber and Taeuber (1958) of the growth and distribution of the United States population. In industrial geography, Geer (1927) was the first to draw attention to the characteristics of the north-eastern manufacturing belt, while regional variations in the level of economic development across the nation were identified and explained by Perloff *et al.* (1960), Odum and Moore (1938), and Caudill (1962). Borchert's (1967) study of metropolitan evolution, Gottmann's (1961) analysis of megalopolis, Murphy and Vance's (1954a, 1954b) investigation of central business districts, and Wirth's (1938) survey of urban lifestyles together accounted for the growth, structure, and character of the nation's cities. In rural areas, Baker (1926) and Weaver (1954) outlined and accounted for the distribution of agricultural production.

These works, and the many others which supplemented them, underlined the importance of centrality, agglomeration, distance decay, and heartland/hinterland in creating a landscape dominated by the industrial metropolis. Taken together, they provide a summary description and explanation of the essential geography of mid-century industrial America.

As manufacturing was the leading sector in industrial society, so the spatial organization of mid-century America was dictated by the location of heavy industry. The principles which determined this pattern are well understood in general terms and involve the initial location of iron and steel production, the key process in the industrial economy, and the associated development of secondary manufacturing in response to agglomerative and linked-process economies. Energy supply, raw material availability, and entrepreneurial skill account for the exceptional concentration of productive capacity in the North-Eastern Seaboard, southern Great Lakes, and Mid-West regions. First recognized by Geer in 1927, and subsequently described and explained in more detail by Hartshorne (1936), Harris (1954), and Pred (1965), this belt housed the basic heavy industry, secondary manufacturing, and related activities of the high mass-consumption economy. The area covered one-eighth of the conterminous United States in 1940, but it held nearly one-half of population and 70 per cent of manufacturing employment. The dominance of the belt is most vividly portrayed by a cartogram in which the area of each state is depicted in proportion to its employment in manufacturing in 1950 (Figure 1.2).

Iron and steel production formed the basic industry in the region. It was located at those points in which basic raw materials could be assembled most cheaply. Major controls on location were exercised by the enormous Appalachians coalfield stretching from West Pennsylvania to Alabama, with its excellent coking coal at Connellsville near Pittsburgh and at Pocahontas in West Virginia, and the iron ores of the Superior Uplands (Figure 1.3). Major centers of steel production included Pittsburgh, Youngstown, and Johnstown on the coalfield, Duluth at the head of Lake Superior, and the break-of-bulk locations of Chicago, Detroit, Cleveland, and Buffalo on the Great Lakes. To these major centers must be added the seventy smaller steel-making towns recognized in the region in 1940 (Warren, 1973).

Associated with iron and steel was a wide range of secondary manufacturing acitivity. By far the most important was motor vehicle production which was concentrated within an "automotive triangle" with apexes at Buffalo, Cincinnati, and Milwaukee, and its center at Detroit. In 1949, this area contained over nine-tenths of the

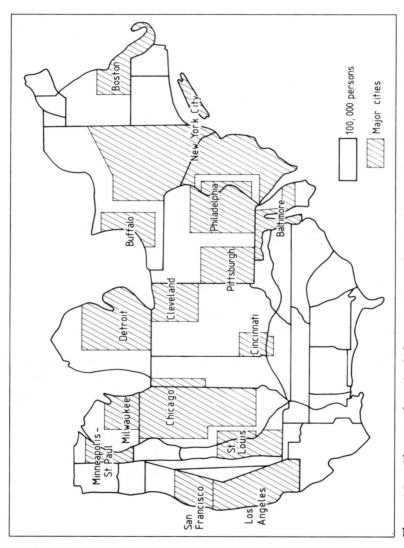

Figure 1.2 *The manufacturing belt, 1950: states and major cities are shown in proportion to their manufacturing employment in 1950*

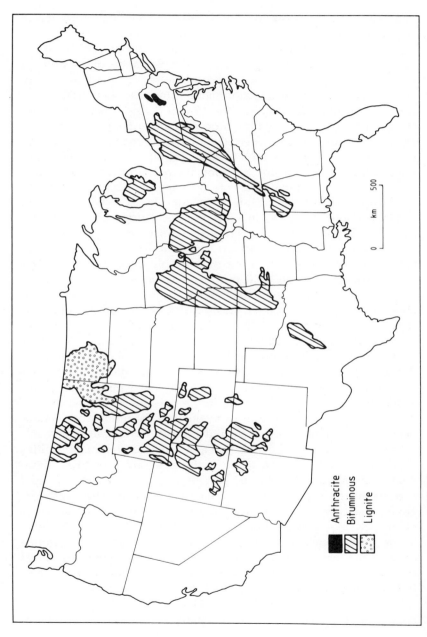

Figure 1.3 *Major coalfields*

nation's automotive employees. Michigan alone accounted for 56 per cent of this number, and Detroit and its suburbs very nearly 40 per cent. Access to steel, the basic resource, and to markets in the north-eastern and central United States explains this distribution in general terms; innovative genius and entrepreneurial skill were specific and critical localization factors. By 1900 there were large numbers of manufacturers in the United States making cars, but there was low output and little product standardization. By designing a simple and durable internal combustion engine and installing it in a single model fabricated by mass-production methods, Henry Ford gave his company and his home town, Detroit, an unassailable early lead in car manufacture. Foremost among those who followed Ford's approach were R.E. Olds of Lansing, Michigan, who launched the Oldsmobile Company in 1901, and W.C Durant of Flint, Michigan, who founded Buick. Geographical concentration was assisted by the existence of very powerful economies of scale in motor vehicle manufacture, which meant that only the very largest companies survived. While total output of vehicles rose rapidly, the number of manufacturers declined sharply. In 1914 there were about 300 motor vehicle firms; in 1923, 103; and in 1927, 44, of which General Motors, Ford, and Chrysler produced about 75 per cent of all cars made. This market share rose to 90 per cent in 1939. This exceptional concentration was both a cause and a consequence of the enormous productive power which was contained in the American manufacturing belt, a pre-eminence perpetuated and sustained by powerful forces of industrial and locational inertia. The existence of the belt in turn testified to the dominant position occupied by manufacturing in mid-century industrial society.

The concentration of population in a small number of large cities was the second major feature of the geography of high mass-consumption America. Urban growth was a comparatively slow process in the pre-industrial mercantilist economy, but, with the emergence of the manufacturing firm with its massive demand for labor, city sizes increased rapidly. For Borchert (1967) a major twist in the spiral of urban growth occurred after 1870 as a consequence of industrialization. With the refinement of steel technology, steel rails replaced iron on both newly built and existing railroads, and heavier equipment, more powerful locomotives, and a standardization of gauges permitted increased speeds, and coast-to-coast shipment of goods. The major consequence of a drastic reduction in the frictional effect of distance was a widening of market areas which provided for the growth of manufacturing centers in the East. Between 1870 and 1920 nearly all the great metropolitan commercial centers of the Mid-West and North-East, while establishing themselves as major industrial cities, retained their positions or advanced one level in the urban hierarchy. The process of population concentration continued and indeed increased after 1920 as a consequence of processes of centralization operating in Borchert's "air, auto, and amenity" epoch. With the introduction of the internal combustion engine in transportation, urban hinterlands were extended further so that central cities grew at the expense of their surrounding regions. Moreover, the tractor, in multiplying the land area the farmer could work by himself, initiated a revolution in farm family size and drastically reduced the level of demand for agricultural labor.

The major beneficiaries of rural depopulation and out-migration were the established metropolitan centers. With the ending of the westward progression of the frontier at the turn of the century, urban growth occurred in places where there were already large concentrations of population. Growth, as Pred (1977) observed, was essentially circular and cumulative, as the population progressively arranged itself into a small number of metropolitan centers. In 1920, 11 per cent of the population lived in Standard Metropolitan Statistical Areas (SMSAs) of over 1 million population, and by 1950, the end of Borchert's epoch, this had risen to 18 per cent. Boom towns of the period included automobile manufacturing centers in the Mid-West, and oilfield cities in Kansas, Oklahoma, Texas, and the Gulf Coast, while the growth of new metropolitan centers in Florida, the South-West, and California, based upon environment and amenity, was indicative of future trends. The aggregate effect of a century of population concentration dictated by the needs of industry was a pattern of settlement in which 95 per cent of the population lived either in central cities or within daily commuting distance in 1950 (Figure 1.4)

The spectacular growth of the largest SMSAs in the air–auto –amenity epoch was responsible by 1960 for the emergence of a super-metropolitan region of 37 million people between Boston and Washington. The unprecedented scale and distinctive character of this urban development was recognized by Gottmann (1961), who, in naming it "Megalopolis", argued that it was in the North-Eastern

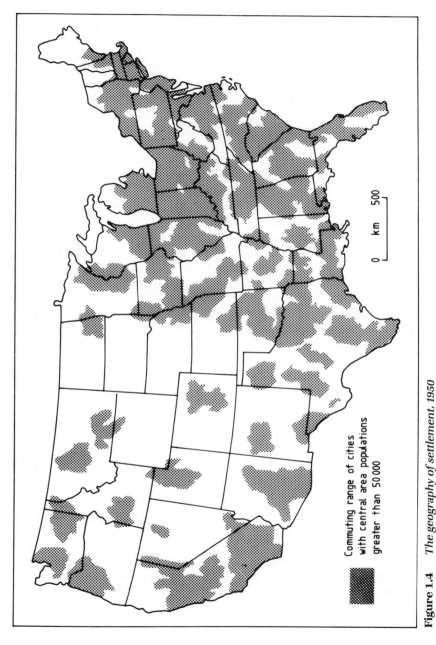

Commuting range of cities
with central area populations
greater than 50 000

0   km   500

Figure 1.4   *The geography of settlement, 1950*

Seaboard of the United States that the ancient Greek dream of a super city was finally realized. In *Megalopolis: The Urbanized Northeastern Seaboard of the United States*, Gottmann painstakingly analyzed the growth and attributes of the region. Alone among urban areas Megalopolis was found to have benefited from processes of concentration dating back to the first days of colonial settlement. It arose as a grouping of the main seaports, commercial centers, and industrial activities in the United States, and to a large extent the maritime facade feature was still recognizable in 1960. Similarly, the manufacturing function has continued and, indeed, a considerable expansion of heavy iron and steel, chemical, and metallurgical industries occurred in the immediate post-war period. Growth in the twentieth century, however, was attributed to the attraction to Megalopolis of a disproportionate share of the nation's financial, political, and industrial decision-making functions. As a consequence, it represented, in 1960, the wealthiest and best-paid concentration of people in the world, and enjoyed a social and cultural pre-eminence reflected in an exceptional assemblage of great universities, libraries, publishing houses, and centers for the visual and performing arts. What made Megalopolis distinctive, however, was not, simply its population size and areal extent, though these were remarkable enough, but the degree to which the constituent SMSAs interacted and interdepended. The commuting areas were not merely contiguous, they overlapped and interlocked in complex ways so that many areas were influenced by more than one city. Secondly, the area was held together by a functional network consisting of a highly varied exchange of people, goods, and ideas. For Gottmann, Megalopolis was rather more than a coalescence of adjacent centers, it was a super-metropolitan system cradling a new order in the organization of inhabited space. In short, it represented the culmination of over a century of processes of population concentration, initiated, maintained, and reinforced by the needs of manufacturing industry and the office-based activities through which that industry was run.

Within the industrial metropolis, the land-use pattern was dominated by a downtown area housing the commercial heart of the industrial economy. Historically, the growth of the Central Business District (CBD) was stimulated first by the railways and then by the construction of networks of radial expressways and developments which successively enhanced the relative accessibility and hence attractiveness of the downtown area. As a consequence, the CBD was the preferred location for divisional and group head offices servicing the corporate empire, for higher order retailing which attracted customers from the furthest reaches of the urban market area, and for those in government and in retailing who provided municipal services and convenience goods for the city residents themselves (Murphy, 1972). Intense competition among these different uses pushed rents to inflated levels so the land value surface both peaked at and declined steeply with distance away from the centre of the CBD. The existence of a compact CBD, with its concentration of skyscraper buildings clustered tightly around the central zone of conflux, symbolized the overriding importance of physical accessibility within the high mass-consumption economy in general, and within the industrial metropolis in particular.

Growth outward from the center meant that the CBD of the industrial metropolis, as observed by Burgess (1925), was surrounded by a set of concentric land use zones, the innermost ring of which contained a large number of old and in many cases obsolete properties (Figure 1.5). Because of subdivision of many units into rooming houses, clearance to create storage areas, and parking lots, and redevelopment for manufacturing and distributive purposes, this zone was an area of mixed residential, commercial,

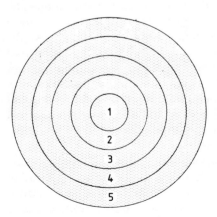

BURGESS' CONCENTRIC ZONES:

1   Central business district

2   Transition zone

3   Independent workingmens homes

4   Better residences

5   Commuter zone

Figure 1.5   *Burgess' concentric zone model of urban social and spatial structure*

wholesaling, and light industrial uses. It was also, typically, the receiving zone and first place of residence for the waves of internal and overseas migrants who streamed into the metropolis in the early years of the twentieth century. Social class characteristically varied with distance away from the center, with the highest status, particularly White professional groups, owning and occupying the most expensive properties on the urban fringe. As the metropolis expanded outwards through the addition of successive zones of suburban development, so properties in the inner ring became progressively downgraded in terms of their perceived desirability. The city at mid-century was surrounded by an extensive commuter belt which encompassed an affluent, mobile, and exurban population. Labor markets were extended furthest by the expressways along which commuters could make most rapid access to the distant city center.

As well as dictating a distinctive geographical order, the industrial metropolis transformed American society. The rural migrants who flocked into the major cities in the early twentieth century soon found that the prevailing social norms, values, and expectations differed fundamentally from those with which they had had previous experience. The city represented an altogether new and different form of economic and social organization. For Wirth (1938), the crowding of large numbers of people from diverse backgrounds into small areas in the city , effectively destroyed existing social and cultural patterns, and created in their place new types of interpersonal relationships and modes of behavior that formed the basis of an urban lifestyle. In contrast to the close-knit, intimate, and stable social relationships which were found in rural society, lifestyles in the rapidly growing early twentieth century metropolis were impersonal, segmental, and transitory. As the size of the city increased, so the possibility of each member of the community knowing all the others personally was reduced. Under these conditions, individuals tended to form only weak links with others so that the close bonds of family and neighborliness, present in rural societies, were replaced by differentiation, specialization, and symbolism. Formal methods of social control by laws, rules, and regulations replaced the informal methods based upon tradition and respect. Indirect communication by letter and telephone replaced personal contacts. Equally important was that the value of social relationships was measured in monetary terms and was manipulated as a means of achieving one's own ends. The effect, for Wirth, was that the status of the individual was debased as he was subsumed as an anonymous member of a social group, responding to institutionalized codes of behavior. Lacking the security provided by familiar norms and sanctions, the individual felt a sense of personal disorganization and loss of identity. Life for many was indeed characterized by "anomie," a condition in which the normal rules which regulate social behavior break down, "alienation", in which the individual becomes detached from society, and social "deviance."

Across the nation, the quality of life at mid-century exhibited pronounced variations. In contrast to the prosperous urban–industrial heartland, large parts of America were either stagnant or were in economic decline. Lagging regions included the South and West with their predominantly resource-based and non-manufacturing economies, while New England, an early center of manufacturing, was experiencing the effects of accelerating de-industrialization. Remoteness from the center was the most important single factor in the regional equation so that the list of most backward areas included large parts of Appalachia, the Ozarks, northern New England, the Upper Great Lakes, the southern coastal plains, and the Four Corners Region.

Economic recession characterized most of the South as a general consequence of several decades of subservience to the Northern economy. Its more specific roots lay in the depressed state of Southern agriculture and the relative absence of industry and urban development, circumstances which gave rise in the first half of the twentieth century to heavy out-migration of population to the North, as Odum and Moore (1938) showed. Most backward of all was the Tennessee Valley, an area of predominantly subsistence farming, with an average per capita income in 1940 which was 45 per cent of the national average. Farms were small and farm families were large so that many individuals who depended upon the land for a living were underemployed. Moreover, industry in the Valley was heavily concentrated in textiles and lumber which paid low wages. So severe in fact was the economic plight of the region that the Tennessee Valley Authority was created in 1933 with the aim of improving flood control, navigation, land reclamation, and reaf-forestation programs which it was hoped would make the area more prosperous agriculturally and more attractive to industry.

Levels of prosperity in non-industrial areas depended in general upon the characteristics of crop production, which in turn reflected the combined effects of physical and economic controls. Patterns of agricultural specialization, mapped by Baker (1926), and outlined in more detail in a series of articles published in *Economic Geography* between 1935 and 1939, were basically dictated by the amounts of effective precipitation and length of growing season, but were distorted in the North-East by the influence of the large and prosperous urban market. As a consequence, dairying predominated in the Great Lakes region, and truck farming of market garden produce and citrus fruits (from Florida) along the east coast, while corn displaced other crops in the corn belt, being used to fatten cattle and hogs for the urban consumer. Though declining in acreage, cotton was still an important crop in the South at mid-century as Prunty (1951) showed. Precipitation levels were critical in the West so that wheat farming and ranching on an extensive basis were the predominant agricultural activities. With irrigation, however, localized production of a range of high value crops was possible in the South-West and in California. Both the value of crops grown and the intensity of land use decreased with distance away from the manufacturing heartland. In consequence, the distributional characteristics of agriculture, like those of industry, population, and regional prosperity reflected the importance of accessibility, centrality, and concentration, the underlying principles which shaped the geography of mid-century high mass-consumption industrial America.

Post-industrial America

Although high mass-consumption industrial society was based upon a powerful and mutually reinforcing set of economic and social relationships, it proved, like its predecessors, to be a comparatively short-lived social formation. Since 1950, a major societal transformation has been unfolding which is gradually ushering America from the industrial to a post-industrial era. The passage into post-industrial society is marked by structural shifts along the same dimensions that distinguished industrial society (Table 1.1). It involves the replacement of one set of social and political relationships by a different configuration. Together these changes amount to the emergence of a new, and fundamentally different, social and economic order.

For Bell, the general form of post-industrial society can be identified by reference to five primary characteristics:

(i)   economic sector: the change from a goods-producing to a service economy

(ii)   occupational distribution: the pre-eminence of the professional and technical class

(iii) axial principle: the centrality of theoretical knowledge as the source of innovation and of policy formulation for society

(iv)   future orientation: the control of technology and technological assessment

(v)   decision making: the creation of a new "intellectual technology."

(Bell 1973, p. 14)

By these criteria, the most obvious characteristic of economic life in the post-industrial society is that the majority of the labor force is

Table 1.2   *Employment by industry, 1950 and 1980*

	1950		1980	
	number (million)	%	number (million)	%
Goods-producing total	26.5	49	31.8	33
Agriculture, forestry, and fishing	6.9	13	3.4	3
Mining	0.9	2	0.9	1
Construction	3.4	6	6.0	6
Manufacturing	15.3	28	21.5	23
Service-producing total	27.8	51	64.9	66
Transportation and utilities	2.9	5	6.3	7
Trade (wholesale and retail)	10.5	19	19.7	20
Finance, insurance, and real estate	1.9	3	5.8	6
Personal, professional, and business services	10.1	20	27.9	28
Public administration	2.4	4	5.2	5

Source: Statistical Abstract of the United States 1954, Table 2401, and 1981, Table 658.

no longer employed in agriculture or manufacturing, but in services (Table 1.2). In 1950, the workforce was evenly balanced between service activities and goods production, but by 1980, the proportion had shifted so that two-thirds were in service industries. Such is their contemporary importance that the major social issues are those of organizing and distributing services. In consequence, the overriding "design" of society is that of a game between people. If industrial society is defined by the quantity of goods as marking a standard of living, the post-industrial society is defined by the quality of life as measured by the services and amenities—health, education, recreation, and the arts—which are deemed to be desirable and possible for all.

The service sector covers many different activities, each of which changed in relative importance during the transformation of industrial to post-industrial America. First, in the very development of industry there was a necessary expansion of transportation and public utilities as auxiliary services in the movement of goods and the increasing use of energy. Second, in the mass consumption of goods and the growth of population there was an increase in distribution (wholesale and retail) and finance, real estate, and insurance. Subsequently, as per capita disposable incomes rose, expenditure on consumer durables, luxury items, and recreation increased. Thus a third group of activities, that of personal services, which includes those working in restaurants, hotels, auto services, travel, entertainment, and sports, began to grow. Full participation in the good life was, however, dependent upon health and education so these areas of provision were next to expand, creating many new jobs in the relevant professions and in government-financed welfare and support services. So wide is the range of services provided in contemporary post-industrial America that it is useful to distinguish the physical services of transportation and utilities in the tertiary sector, the financial services including trade, insurance, and real estate in the quaternary sector, and quinary sector ideas and information services. Official statistics do not enable the size of these sectors to be identified with precision, but about a quarter of the workforce are employed in quaternary sector activities. A further 15 per cent are in the quinary sector.

The size of the quinary sector is the most important indicator of the progression into post-industrialism. As information replaces energy as the key resource, so those whose jobs involve the creation, storage, and dissemination of ideas increase in number and relative importance. Foremost among the information service workers are those employed in health care and education which constitute two of the growth "industries" in the United States. Over 9 million were employed in hospitals and health services in the United States in 1980, and 7 million in elementary, secondary, and college education. The demands for more extensive and improved services, especially in the areas of health and education, are causes of a sizable expansion in government employment. Similarly, the inadequacy of the market in meeting the needs for a decent environment leads to an increase in the level of government intervention and regulation which produces a further increase in jobs. Over 16 million people were on state and federal government payrolls in 1980.

Related to the expansion of employment in services is the rise to pre-eminence of the professional and technical class of doctors, teachers, research workers, scientists, and engineers. As a group in the labor force, they are distinguished not so much by their white-collar status as by graduate and post-graduate education and professional qualifications. In 1940 there were 3.9 million such persons in the United States; by 1960 the number had risen to 7.5

Table 1.3   *Occupation of employed workers, 1960 and 1980*

	1960 number (million)	%	1980 number (million)	%
White-collar workers	28.5	43	50.8	52
Professional and technical	7.5	11	15.6	16
Managers and administrators	7.0	11	10.9	11
Salesworkers	4.2	6	6.2	6
Clerical workers	9.8	15	18.1	19
Blue-collar workers	24.0	37	30.8	32
Craft and kindred workers	8.6	14	12.6	13
Operatives	11.9	18	13.8	14
Non-farm laborers	3.5	5	4.4	5
Service workers	8.0	12	12.9	13
Farm workers	5.1	8	2.7	3

Source: Statistical Abstract of the United States 1981, Table 673.

million and by 1980 was 15.6 million, making it the second largest of the eight occupational divisions in the country, exceeded only by clerical workers (Table 1.3). Between 1940 and 1980 the growth rate of the professional and technical class was twice that of the labor force as a whole, but the growth rate of scientists and engineers was triple that of the working population. In 1978, the United States had 1.3 million scientists as opposed to 0.3 million in 1940. As a consequence of the rise of the meritocracy, the university research institute has joined the business firm as a major social focus in society.

In contrast to industrial society, which is concerned with the co-ordination of men and machines for the production of goods, post-industrial society is organized around knowledge for the purpose of social control and the direction of innovation and change. What is distinctive is indeed the centrality of *theoretical* knowledge, the primacy of theory over empiricism. Theory provides the basis for management of industry and the economy, and is the springboard for the development of new products and processes. Rather than the fortuitous inventions and *ad hoc* adaptations that characterized the industrial era, post-industrial technology is advanced by translating theoretical principles into practical applications.

The increasing emphasis placed upon theoretical science is illustrated by the growth of expenditure on research and development (R & D) which increased from 1.5 per cent of gross national product in 1955 to 2.4 per cent in 1981. At 3 billion dollars in 1955, federal defense and space-related expenditure equaled all other forms of basic and applied R & D, but the amount in 1981 was 48.3 billion dollars. The pay-off from R & D investment of this magnitude is reflected by the growth of the science-based industries of polymers and artificial fibers, optics, electronics, computers, aerospace, drugs, and biotechnology products. These industries have eclipsed iron and steel, automobile and aeronautical engineering, and shipbuilding, and are increasingly dominating the manufacturing sector. Moreover, as science provides the key to economic progress, the role of the universities and research institutes in post-industrial society is further enhanced.

The contribution of theoretical science and research and development to innovation and change is shown by the computer industry, one of the leading sectors in the information-oriented

post-industrial economy. Although designs for an electromech-
anical calculating machine were published by Babbage in the early
nineteenth century, the modern electronic computer traces its
origins to research projects funded by the United States federal
government at a number of universities in the 1940s. These cul-
minated in the construction of the Electronic Numerical Integrator
and Calculator (ENIAC) at the University of Pennsylvania in 1946 for
governmental, primarily military, use. The experience gained on
this project enabled a number of the research workers involved to
set up their own company to produce the UNIVAC 1 (Universal
Automatic Computer), the first commercial version of which was
delivered in 1954. Subsequent developments in science and technology have taken the computer industry through four generations
based upon valves (1945–54), transistors (1954–65), integrated cir-
cuits (1965–78), and large-scale integrators (LSIs) or micro-
processors from 1972 onwards. In consequence, the number of

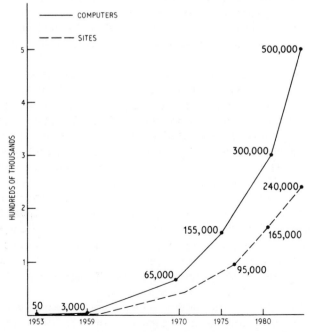

Figure 1.6   *Growth in the number of computers in the United States*

computers in use in the United States has risen exponentially over the last thirty years (Figure 1.6). The development cycle, which involves initial government funding at an academic institution leading to commercial applications, is similar to that experienced in the aerospace, electronics, and biotechnology industries. Theoretical knowledge has replaced *ad hoc* experimentation as the determinant of economic progress.

Bell's fourth distinguishing characteristic is the increased emphasis which is placed upon the planning of technology. Whereas industrial society grew through investment in production techniques, in a spontaneous and largely unpredictable manner, the success of post-industrial technology is closely linked to its ability to minimize uncertainty by planning for the future. Emphasis is therefore placed upon guiding the course of technology and regulating its expansion through the deployment of resources and investment. Technology is seen as an economic product that can be created in the same way as manufactured goods. The use of techniques of extrapolation and forecasting to predict developments in technology enables firms to orient themselves towards the future, thereby speeding up the process of industrial change. Some indication of the increasing pace of technological change is seen in the reduction in the time lag between technological innovation and commercial manufacture. This was, according to Servan-Schreiber (1968), 112 years for photography (1727 to 1839), 56 years for the telephone (1820 to 1876), 35 years for radio (1867 to 1902), 15 years for radar (1925 to 1940), 12 years for television (1922 to 1934), 5 years for the transistor (1948 to 1953), and 3 years for the integrated circuit (1958 to 1961). The planning of technology is merely one aspect of a more general concern for the future that characterizes post-industrial society. This is seen in the growth of planning as a function of both state and federal government.

The final dimension refers to a fundamental change in the ways in which decisions are made. For Bell, the major intellectual and sociological problems of the post-industrial society are those of "organized complexity," the management of large-scale systems with large numbers of interacting variables which have to be co-ordinated to achieve specific goals. Since 1940 he identifies a remarkable proliferation of new fields of inquiry whose results apply to problems of organized complexity: information theory, cybernetics, decision theory, game theory, utility theory, and stochastic modeling. From these have come a range of techniques which are used to predict alternative optimal outcomes of different choices. Taken together, these applications amount to the development of an "intellectual technology," a set of problem-solving rules and procedures which has replaced intuitive judgment as the basis for decision making. The rules may be embodied in a program or in a complex mathematical formula. The computer is indeed a critical development for, without it, simultaneous consideration of large numbers of interacting variables would be impossible. Intellectual technology increasingly provides the means of making judgments about, and managing, the complex social and economic systems which characterize post-industrial society.

Taken together, changes in economic structure, occupational distribution, the role of theoretical knowledge, the emphasis placed upon the future, and the importance of decision making, point to the progressive replacement of mid-century industrialism by a new and different social formation. Although each development can be looked at individually, in combination they define the major facets of emerging post-industrialism. As well as the breadth and depth of change, it is important to emphasize the time period involved, for a structural shift of this magnitude has taken place in the long term, over several decades, rather than merely in a few years. As such, it is only loosely related to medium-term swings in the level of economic activity which are associated with the Kondratieff cycle (Rostow, 1977). It is largely unconnected with short-term fluctuations in activity as represented, for example, by the succession of the boom of the 1960s by the recession of the 1970s. Although this particular reversal was of a seriousness sufficient to suggest that the Golden Economic Age was gone forever (Allvine and Tarpley, 1977) and that the Age of Austerity had arrived (Claval *et al.*, 1980), its causes were specific, related to oil price rises, rather than structural in origin. "Slow growth" undoubtedly has some geographical consequences as Phillips and Brunn (1978) observe, but the massive redistributions of population, industry, agricultural production, and urban and regional activity which have occurred in the United States since mid-century are the product of deep-seated rather than ephemeral changes in the structure of the economy and society.

Despite the logic of Bell's arguments, and their detailed empirical support, the concepts of the industrial and post-industrial societies can be criticized on a number of grounds. The first is diagnostic and focuses upon the structural dimensions which are used to distinguish and name the two social formations. While not questioning the fact that a new social and economic pattern has emerged in America in the post-war period, several observers have played down the role of industry as the primary determinant and index of change. Instead, they have underlined the importance of shifts in the nature of economic structure, capital, technology, and consumption. Thus in place of post-industrialism, Rostow (1965) prefers "post maturity," Dahrendorf (1959) and Mandel (1975) suggest "post capitalist," and Brzezinski (1970) introduces the term "techneotronic." In looking towards the year 2000, Kahn and Weiner (1967) depict a society so affluent that work and efficiency have lost their contemporary meaning. Rather than post-industrial, this suggests that "post-economic" might be more appropriate. Although these contributions highlight very different aspects of the contemporary social formation, they are not, however, necessarily incompatible with the broad concept of the post-industrial society. The progression from industrialism to post-industrialism is accompanied by major changes across a wide range of dimensions, the relative importance of which raises questions of emphasis and interpretation. As a general conceptual scheme, the post-industrial society accommodates and encompasses a variety of more specialized viewpoints on the primary characteristics of the contemporary social formation.

A second reservation relates to variations in the level of socio-economic development across the United States which mean that the concept of the post-industrial society cannot be applied equally to all areas. Rather than view the economy as an integrated whole which has progressed uniformly from industrialism to post-industrialism, the country must be seen as a set of regional economies, each at a different stage of development. Since the colonial period, the North-Eastern Seaboard has played a major role of innovation and change, a role now additionally performed by California, whereas large parts of the South, especially Appalachia, the North-West and the High Plains, have lagged behind. In consequence, the progression to post-industrialism is highly pronounced in some regions, while elements of traditional social and economic structures, which owe much to the influence of the industrial era, remain elsewhere. The nature of change within post-industrial society, however, is such that these historical differentials are progressively being broken down. Indeed, some of the major geographical consequences of contemporary information and transportation technologies arise out of their contribution to regional integration. Complete uniformity in levels of economic and social development do not yet exist across the nation, but such variations as remain are insufficient to seriously undermine the description of contemporary America as a post-industrial society.

Conclusion

The preceding arguments and observations suggest that a type of society has emerged and is emerging in the United States which is fundamentally different to that which existed at mid-century. Increased service activity, white-collar employment, high-techno-logy industry, and expenditure on research and development, are among the most obvious indices of change, reflecting a basic reordering in the structure of society. As a corollary, technological innovation, based upon developments in scientific theory, and decision making have enhanced importance. To these economic developments must be added the changes of attitudes, expecta-tions and aspirations, in part determined by increased levels of education, leisure, and affluence, which reflect and define a shifting social consciousness. Such changes are less tangible, but are equally far-reaching, and include the rise of secularism and human-ism, and the erosion of work-oriented, achievement-oriented and advancement-oriented values (Kahn and Weiner, 1967). These eco-nomic and social developments are both interlinked and self-reinforcing. Taken together, they are indicative of the rise of a new and distinctive social formation.

Structural changes on this scale have inevitable and profound consequences for the geography of the United States. A different set of locational principles supporting a new geographical order may be expected in accordance with the requirements of a prosperous service-and-technology-oriented, white-collar dominated, informa-tion-and-research-based society. In consequence, new distribu-tions of population, employment, regional advantage, and interac-tion can be expected to replace those dictated by the preceding social formation. As the geography of the pre-industrial mercantilist economy was replaced by spatial patterns determined by the needs of the high mass-consumption industrial society, so these in turn are being succeeded by a locational order imposed by post-industrial society.

Against this background of change, succeeding chapters outline this geography. Many of the constituent patterns are embryonic and some are merely suggestive, as post-industrial society is an evolving rather than an established social formation, but together they combine and reinforce one another in ways which herald a radical departure from that established in the industrial era. The extent of change can be measured against the geography of the United States at mid-century, indeed a comparison of patterns in 1950 and 1980 is the basic methodology adopted in this book. Against this background, Chapter 3 examines the emerging geography of industry and employment, Chapter 4 looks at the post-industrial city, while Chapter 5 explores the extent of recent geographical changes in agriculture. Chapter 6 is concerned with geographical consequences of societal change at the regional scale. Having outlined the characteristics of industrial and post-industrial America in general terms, it is now appropriate to explore the implications of change on the growth and distribution of the population.

2

The changing distribution of population

The preceding chapter outlined and summarized the essential economic and social characteristics of industrial and post-industrial America. Deep-seated shifts in the character and role of industry, employment, science, and technology are indicative of a fundamental reorientation of economy and society away from goods production and towards service provision. In consequence, the contemporary social formation in the United States differs markedly from that at mid-century. Historical precedents suggest that structural changes on this scale both give rise to, and are made possible by, profound changes in the spatial organization and arrangement of social and economic activities. In consequence, a new geographical order is evolving which affects and accommodates the needs and requirements of the emerging post-industrial age.

Foremost among the consequences of the rise of post-industrialism are the effects of structural change upon the growth and distribution of population. The most noticeable trend concerns overall population, for although the number of Americans continues to rise, the rate of growth has slowed appreciably in recent years. This change is largely attributable to a decline in birth rate such that the rate of natural increase today is below replacement level. As a consequence, internal migration has become a major determinant of geographical variations in population size and growth. Generally, the South and West are expanding whereas the North-East is stagnating; California, Florida, and Texas are exceptional in terms of their record of post-war growth. At the local level, non-metropolitan areas and the outer limits of commuter fields are growing at the expense of city centers and suburbs.

These spatial shifts amount to a progressive break-up of the clusters of population in the urban manufacturing states of the North-East that dominated the population map of industrial America. Rather than locate in increasing numbers in the industrial heartland and in the major cities, the population is deconcentrating on a massive scale. These redistribution processes reflect in part an element of regional convergence in that the West and South are progressively "catching-up," but the scale of the population losses experienced by the North-East since the early 1970s suggest that powerful structural forces are now compounding long-term trends. At the local level, deconcentration amounts to "counter-urbanization," a process through which urban populations are dispersing. Reflected over a wider area than suburbanization, the evidence is that people are being drawn to small towns and rural areas in increasing numbers. For Berry (1975, p. 180), the combined pattern is one of growth "in the amenity rich locations of the western and southern 'rimland' on a national scale, and also at and beyond the edge of Standard Metropolitan Statistical Areas as the Census Bureau defines them, on a regional scale." The emerging geography of population in post-industrial America is almost the exact opposite of the highly concentrated and centralized regional and urban patterns identified and analyzed by Taeuber and Taeuber (1958) at mid-century.

Explanations of these geographical shifts lie in people's responses to environmental and economic opportunity. They reflect the attractions of sunbelt and rural environments in terms of amenity, climate, and access to unspoiled countryside; and a rejection of aged, obsolescent, and decaying urban industrial areas with their accelerating social and economic problems. Technology is also important and has given locational freedom to an ever-widening cross-section of post-industrial society. Transport and communication improvements have created the means whereby people can readily respond to their location preferences through movement. These simplifications about patterns, trends, and causes, however, conceal the many subtleties of demographic change that combine to create the emerging population geography of post-industrial America. In view of these complexities, it is useful to examine the dynamics of population change and distribution at national, state, and local levels.

Population growth

The most important feature of the recent demography of the United States concerns the size and rates of national population increase. Since 1950, 75 million people have been added to the United States population so that there were 227 million Americans in 1980. This made the United States the fourth most populous country in the world after China (1041 million), India (708 million) and the USSR (268 million). Despite this impressive gain, the rate of population increase has slowed appreciably in recent years. Between 1950 and 1960, the rate of expansion was 18.5 per cent. It was 11.4 per cent over the period 1970 to 1980 (Table 2.1). Even with this modest rate of growth, 2 million, that is the equivalent of a city the size of Philadelphia, are being added to the population each year. This increase is significantly less, however, than was expected at mid-century. It is far below the "high fertility" projection of the Bureau of Census report *200 million Americans* published as recently as 1967, which gave a population of 250 million by 1980. Indeed it is slightly below the Bureau's projected "low fertility" figure of 228 million. Since 1972, the intrinsic rate of natural population change, that is the projected long-term rate adjusted for age structure, has in fact been negative, indicating that without immigration the population would be in decline. The leveling off in the rate of population increase is one of the most important correlates of the rise of post-industrialism. Population projection is a notoriously difficult science but current trends in fertility, combined with the progression of the post Second World War "baby boom" generation beyond peak child-bearing age, suggest a continuing slowdown in the rate of growth by the year 2000.

In accounting for the recent pattern of population growth, it is

Table 2.1 *Selected demographic statistics*

	Resident population	Increase over preceding census		Vital statistics			
	Number (million)	Number (million)	%	Birth rate (births/000)	Death rate (deaths/000)	Immigrants admitted (million)	Intrinsic rate of natural increase[1]
1950	151.3	19.1	14.5	24.1	9.6	0.24	16.8
1960	179.3	28.0	18.5	23.7	9.5	0.26	18.6
1970	203.3	24.0	13.4	18.4	9.5	0.37	6.0
1980	226.5	23.2	11.4	15.9	8.7	0.46	−6.0

Note: The intrinsic rate of natural increase is the rate that would eventually prevail if the population were to experience, at each year of age, the birth rates and death rates occurring in the specified year and if those rates remained unchanged over a long period of time.

Source: Statistical Abstract of the United States 1981, Tables 1, 84, 85, 108, and 129.

necessary to comment on the movements of the three relevant variables, birth rate, death rate, and immigration. By far the most important is the dramatic decline in the birth rate, which fell by one-third between 1950 and 1980 (Table 2.1). At an average of 15.2 for the last five years of the 1970s, the number of births per thousand population was lower than at any time this century. In contrast, the change in death rate over the post-war period, though downward, has been marginal and has had little overall effect on the size of the population. The net effect of immigration, however, has increased significantly since 1950 and at half a million a year is currently at its highest level since the introduction of quotas in 1929. Though small in comparison with nineteenth century levels, immigration is responsible for a quarter of the current annual population increase and so is a significant factor in determining the overall size and character of the United States population.

Birth rates have fallen because an increasing number of women both prefer and are able to have fewer children. The desire to remain childless or to limit the number of offspring reflects important changes in the status, role, and behavior of women that are products of the more widespread availability of consumerist, careerist, and high leisure lifestyles in post-industrial society. Presented with these alternatives, fewer women are prepared to commit themselves exclusively to traditional familism in which the main emphasis is upon child producing and child rearing. Instead, there is an increased preference for remaining single, for delaying marriage, for divorce and remarriage, for having fewer children, and for combining child rearing with a job. Particularly significant is the divorce rate, which more than doubled from 2.2 to 5.4 divorces and annulments per 1000 population between 1960 and 1980. Similarly, the number of single (never married) females increased from 12 to 17 per cent of the total population over the same period. The precise influences of these individual social trends upon fertility levels are difficult to specify since they are both causes and consequences of changing attitudes towards children and the family. Together they contribute to a set of circumstances in which women today expect to have fewer children than women at mid-century.

The fact that family sizes can be regulated has been made possible by use of increasingly well-developed and widely accepted methods of birth control. Especially important is the contraceptive pill which must be regarded as one of the most socially influential products of post-industrial biomedical technology. First developed and introduced by the pharmaceutical company G.D. Searle, as a result of research undertaken by George Pincus at the Worcester Foundation for Experimental Biology up to 1955, it is currently the choice of a quarter of the 70 per cent of American women of child-bearing age who regularly use contraception. A contributory factor was the legalization of abortion, first in New York in 1970 and then in the nation in 1973. In 1978 there were on average 417 legal abortions for every 1000 live births in the USA and abortions actually exceeded live births in the District of Columbia.

Looking towards the future, the United States Census in 1975 identified three possible courses of population increase to the end of the century. (US Bureau of Census, 1975). Starting from a population of 214 million in 1975, the Bureau projected, on the low side, 245 million on the basis of 1.7 children per woman; 263 million at 2.1 children per woman; and 287 million at 2.7 children per woman. Even the highest of these projections, 287 million, is well below the 361 million forecast by the Bureau in 1960. The actual increase of population between 1950 and 1975 was 62 million. Even the middle estimate suggests that the increase between 1975 and 2000 will be less than 50 million. For Watson (1982, p. 311), the reasons for a continuing reduction in the rate of population increase are many and varied:

> (i) fewer women will marry; (ii) more women will carry on longer in their education; (iii) women will marry later at 23–26; (iv) married women will continue in their careers for longer (5 years or more); (v) women will have their first child later, at 28–32; (vi) more women will be divorced; (vii) more divorces will take place before having children; this will postpone the first child; (viii) more women will have a second divorce, delaying their chances of having children or at least a second child; (viii) more divorcees will go back to their careers and will not remarry, thus having no children.

As well as these effects of changing marriage practices, Watson points to the increasing importance of regulating family size so as to maintain high personal standards of living, the likely effects of the availability of abortion on demand, and the growing climate of opinion among women with stable marriages in favor of no-child or one-child households. A final factor is the trend among many young couples to live in apartment blocks where there is not the space for raising a family. Acting together these factors seem likely to reduce still further the rate of population increase over the next fifteen years.

The changing geography of population

The overriding feature of the changing population geography is the recent reversal in the long-term regional patterns of population growth. By virtue of its early settlement and exceptional resource endowment, the North-Eastern manufacturing belt states have long been dominant as centers of population. Growth has occurred from year to year since the early eighteenth century on account of natural increases and net immigration. In the last decade, however, this established pattern has been broken as the manufacturing belt has undergone an absolute decline. This reversal underlines the diminishing importance of manufacturing activities as determinants of the distribution and growth of population in post-industrial society. For purposes of analyzing the evolving distribution of population it is convenient to use the system of regions, divisions, and states for which statistics are assembled and published by the Bureau of Census (Figure 2.1). The overall pattern of shifts is summarized in Table 2.2 which underlines the very different population growth performance of the North-East and North Central Regions as compared with the South and West. Between 1950

Table 2.2 *Population of the United States by census region, 1950–80*

| Region | Population in millions | | Increase 1950–80 | |
	1950	1980	Millions	%
North-East	39.5	49.1	9.6	24.3
North Central	44.5	58.9	14.4	32.4
South	47.2	75.3	28.1	59.6
West	20.2	43.2	23.0	113.9
USA				49.6

Source: Statistical Abstract of the United States 1981, Table 9.

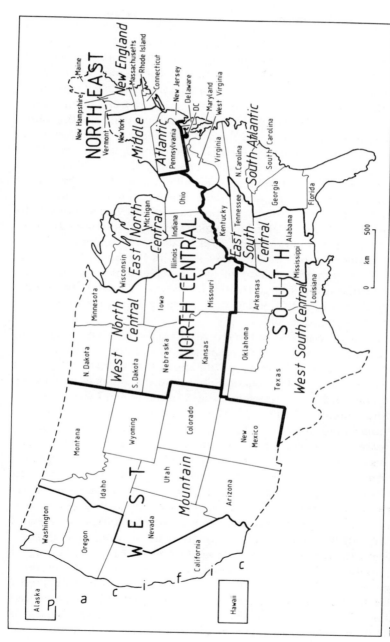

Figure 2.1   *States, regions, and divisions*

and 1980 the latter two grew more rapidly in both absolute and relative terms, with the West expanding especially vigorously. In part this difference reflects the long-term redistribution of people as underlined by the progressive shift in the center of gravity of population in the conterminous United States. In 1980 it was for the first time located west of the Mississippi (Figure 2.2). That this point still lies some distance east of the geographical center of the nation (which is in Kansas) is because of the heavy concentrations of population in the states of the manufacturing belt, especially New York (17.6 million), Pennsylvania (11.8 million), and Illinois (11.4 million) (Figure 2.3). In contrast, populations in the Prairies, High Plains, mountain states, and in large parts of the South, are small. Forty-five per cent of the population west of the Mississippi is to be found in two states: California, which with 23.6 million is the most populous state in the Union, and Texas (14.3 million). It is the growth performance of the larger states in the North-East, South, and West, rather than that of the sparsely settled states of the interior that register large relative increases on small base populations, that primarily defines the emerging human geography of post-industrial America.

Because of variations in the growth of population within the post-war period, it is useful to compare patterns of population increase over two periods, 1950 to 1970, and 1970 to 1980. The most noticeable feature of population change at the states level between 1950 and 1970 is the spectacular and unparalleled increase recorded by California (Figure 2.4). The 9.4 million which were added to its population amounted to 18 per cent of the total population increase in the United States as a whole over the twenty year period. So exceptional was the growth of California that it completely outstripped its southern rivals, Florida (4.0 million) and Texas (3.5 million). Although much attention has, rightly, focused on these three growth phenomena, several states in the north also recorded significant increases. New York alone gained 3.4 million people and so confirmed its continuing attraction as an area of residence. Major additions were also recorded by Ohio (2.7 million), Michigan (2.5 million), Illinois (2.4 million), and New Jersey (2.3 million). Together with New York and tiny Connecticut (which still gained 1 million), they defined a cluster of contiguous, highly populated states which, up to 1970, were year by year adding continually to their totals. The importance of the manufacturing belt may have

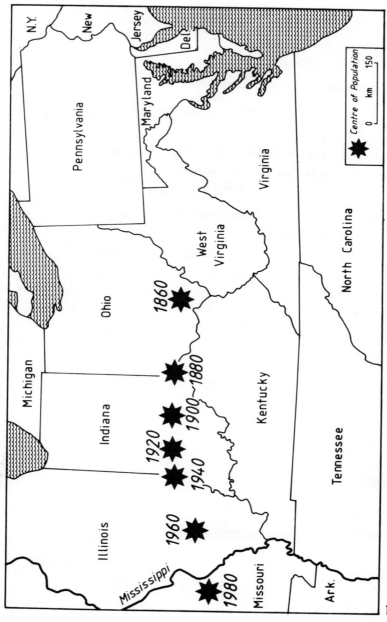

Figure 2.2 *The changing center of gravity of population*

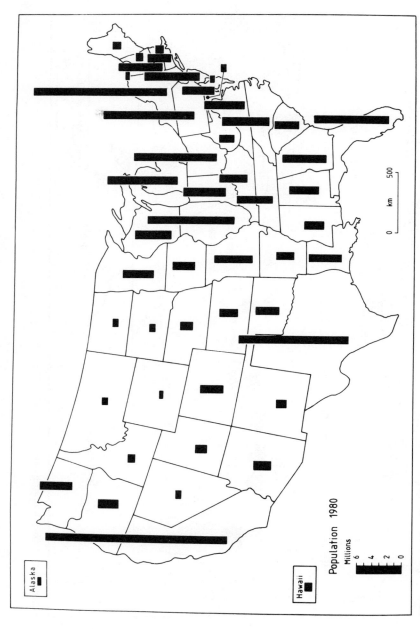

Figure 2.3 *The distribution of population, 1980*

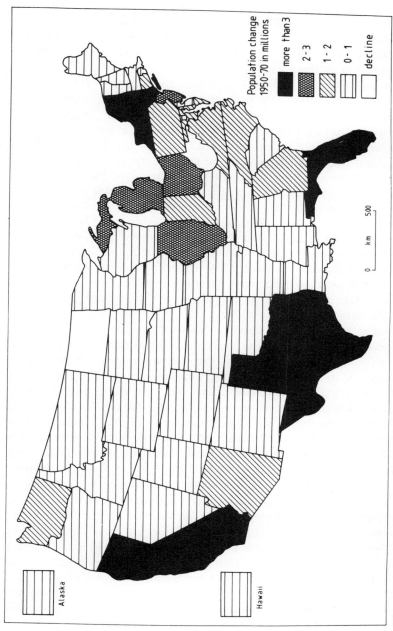

Population change
1950–70 in millions

more than 3

2 - 3

1 - 2

0 - 1

decline

Alaska

Hawaii

Figure 2.4 *Population change, 1950–70*

been diminished in relative terms on account of the expansion of California, Texas, and Florida, but it grew impressively up to 1970 in absolute terms and still contained the largest concentration of population in the nation.

In contrast to these cases of growth, the majority of the states in the interior achieved modest gains. North Dakota, West Virginia, and the District of Columbia actually declined in population between 1950 and 1970, while, with increases of less than 100,000, Maine, Vermont, Iowa, South Dakota, Mississippi, Arkansas, Wyoming, and Montana were virtually static. Very small absolute and relative increases were indeed recorded by all of the states of the West North Central and East South Central Divisions, showing that the Prairies and the Old South remained, over the period, relatively unattractive to settlers. Nevada, Colorado, Arizona, and Alaska are in a different category in that they added modest numbers to small base populations and so achieved rates of increase in excess of twice the national average. They underline the emergence of the West in general and the South-West in particular as areas of growth which may be expected to contain increasingly large populations by the end of the century.

Since 1970, census statistics show that some profound and fundamental changes have taken place in the geographical pattern of population growth. By far the most important is the major downturn in the fortunes of the manufacturing belt states which were growing so impressively over the preceding twenty years, indeed over the preceding two centuries (Figure 2.5). New York, which was the fourth ranking state in terms of total additions to its population between 1950 and 1970, actually lost two-thirds of a million people between 1970 and 1980 and joined Rhode Island and the District of Columbia in the list of states in absolute decline. More detailed statistics show that 1971 was in fact the year of peak population for New York and in each year since the state has lost an average of 90,000 people. Despite their similar pre-1970 performances, Ohio, Pennsylvania, and New Jersey fared little better, registering only very small increases. None of these states gained more than a quarter of a million over the decade and, together with Illinois and Massachusetts, all have declined in population since 1978. These reversals mean that the 1970s mark a major turning point in the regional development of the United States. During the decade, manufacturing belt states, whose size, growth, and special-

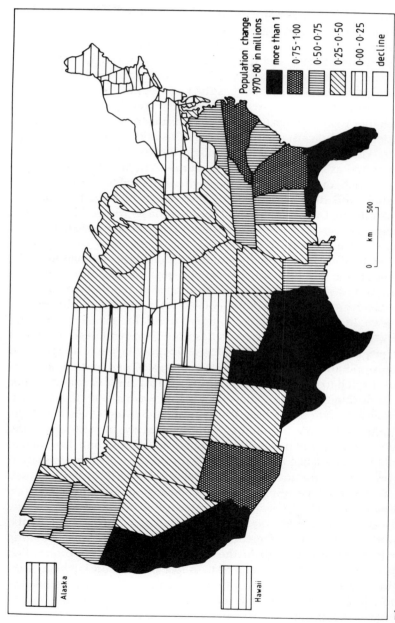

Figure 2.5   *Population change, 1970–80*

isms had hitherto dominated the human geography of the United States, entered a period of absolute as well as relative decline.

In contrast, Figure 2.5 shows that states in the South have undergone a recent revival. Louisiana, Alabama, Tennessee, and the Carolinas emerged in the last census decade as major growth areas. Their performance since 1970 is the exact opposite of that between 1950 and 1970 during which time they were virtually stagnant. Together with Virginia, Georgia, and Florida, these states comprise a region of significant population increases and rapid rates of expansion. Florida alone gained 2.9 million between 1970 and 1980 and expanded at four times the national rate. The picture elsewhere is very much one of growth-on-growth, with California gaining 3.6 million and Texas 3.0 million. Despite small base populations, Washington, Oregon, Colorado, and Arizona increased by over half a million over the decade so underlining the continued expansion of the West and South-West.

Regional variations in the rates of population change are mirrored in the growth performance of metropolitan areas across the nation. Indeed it is change in the number of people living in cities that is the primary determinant of each state's demographic performance. In common with the national trend, the overall population of American metropolitan areas has undergone a marked change in recent years. Throughout the 1950s, the growth rate of all Standard Metropolitan Statistical Areas (SMSAs) was 2.6 per cent per annum, but this fell to 1.7 per cent per annum during the 1960s, and 1.2 per cent during the 1970s. Especially notable was the slowing down in the growth rate of the largest urban units. Between 1960 and 1970, SMSAs with over 3 million population grew by 11.9 per cent. Between 1970 and 1980, they declined by 0.5 per cent. The metropolitan system, like the nation, is nearing a state of zero population growth as Brunn and Wheeler (1980) and Rust (1975) have shown.

This overall pattern, however, conceals some pronounced regional contrasts in sizes and rates of urban growth. A basic distinction can again be drawn between the North-East and the South and West for, whereas the northern metropolis is stagnating or is in decline, growth in the cities of the sunbelt is proceeding apace (Figure 2.6). Nineteen SMSAs lost population between 1970 and 1980 and, with the exception of St Louis, all are old established industrial centers located at the heart of the manufacturing belt. In contrast, 54 of the 172 SMSAs with populations of 200,000 or more

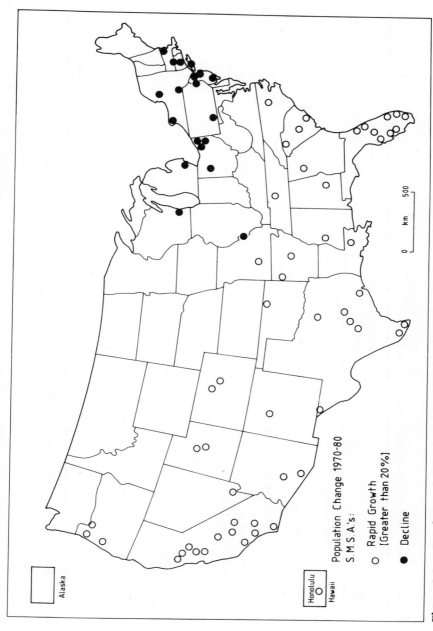

Figure 2.6 *Population change by Standard Metropolitan Statistical Area, 1970–80*

Table 2.3 *Population change in metropolitan areas, 1970–80*

Metropolitan area	Population (000s) 1980	Population change 1970–80 Number (000s)	Population change 1970–80 %
Greatest absolute increases			
Houston	2905	906	45
Dallas–Fort Worth	2975	597	25
Phoenix	1508	537	55
Anaheim–Santa Ana–Garden Grove	1932	511	36
San Diego	1862	504	37
Tampa–St Petersburg	1569	480	44
Los Angeles–Long Beach	7478	436	6
Atlanta	2030	434	27
Riverside–San Bernardino–Ontario	1557	418	37
Fort Lauderdale–Hollywood	1014	394	64
Greatest absolute losses			
New York	9120	−854	−9
Cleveland	1899	−165	−8
Pittsburgh	2264	−137	−6
Boston	2763	−136	−5
Philadelphia	4714	−107	−2
Buffalo	1243	−101	−8

Source: Statistical Abstract of the United States 1981, Table 23.

recorded population growth rates in excess of 20 per cent. All are in the South or West, and the majority are in the sunbelt strip which extends from the Carolinas, through Florida, and along the Gulf Coast and Mexican border to include southern California. Nine metropolitan areas in the South and West gained more than 400,000 population over the period 1970–80, and Houston, Dallas–Fort Worth, Phoenix, Anaheim–Santa Ana–Garden Grove, and San Diego all increased by over half a million. With a 62 per cent increase, Fort Lauderdale–Hollywood was the fastest growing of the nation's metropolitan areas and a further eight of the biggest gainers in absolute terms also recorded rates of increase in excess of 25 per cent. Conversely, New York, with a decline of 854,000, dominates the list of six metropolitan areas which lost over 100,000 population over the decade (Table 2.3). All are urban industrial centers in the North-East which maintained steady rates of growth up to the mid-sixties. The differences between 1950–70 and 1970–80 at both state and metropolitan levels underline in general the declining influence of traditional manufacturing activities upon the growth and distribution of population. They reflect the range of locational responses to the structural changes that are implicit in the progression from industrial to post-industrial society.

Components of change

As at the national level, detailed explanations of these trends and patterns are best approached by way of analysis of births, deaths, and the effects of migration. The first two can usefully be combined by subtracting deaths from births to produce a figure for the natural increase of the population. Mapping values for each state reveals some important regional contrasts which in part account for geographical variations in overall population growth (Figure 2.7). The rate of natural increase was consistently high through the South and West over the period 1950–70, being over 50 per cent in the case of New Mexico, Arizona, Utah, and Nevada. Conversely, it was low in the North-East and in the continental interior. These differences are primarily attributable to the birth rate which varies widely across the nation with extremes in 1979 of 30.1 live births per 1000 population in Utah to 12.2 per 1000 in Massachusetts. Death rates range more narrowly from 4.1 per 1000 in Alaska to 10.2 per 1000 in Pennsylvania. Differences in the birth rate reflect the age

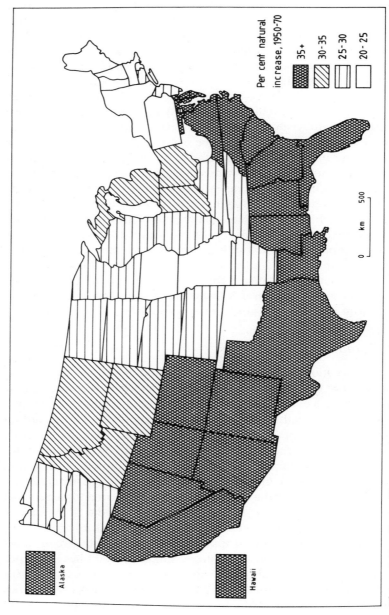

Figure 2.7   *Natural increase in population, 1950–70*

distribution of states' populations together with the influence of ethnicity and culture. Especially critical are contrasting attitudes towards family size and willingness to use contraception, between Whites, Blacks, Spanish Americans, and Indians, and between Protestants, Catholics, and Mormons.

To the growth resulting from natural increases must be added or subtracted the effects of net migration. It is here that the primary explanation for the dramatic downturn in the fortunes of the manufacturing belt states, and the revival of the South, lies. Between 1950 and 1970, the eight major manufacturing states in the North— Connecticut, New York, New Jersey, Pennsylvania, Ohio, Indiana, Illinois, and Michigan—together gained 1 million population as a consequence of net migration (Figure 2.8). In the five-year period 1970–5, they lost 1.8 million (Figure 2.9). Conversely, in the South, Kentucky, Tennessee, Mississippi, Alabama, Georgia, and the Carolinas lost 3 million over the twenty years up to 1970, but gained 0.5 million in the five years after. Migrational flows to the east of the Mississippi since 1970 are almost the exact opposite in direction of those identified and analyzed by Bogue in 1959. Net out-migration is reducing the population of manufacturing belt states by as many as are added annually through natural increase, thereby producing stagnation and decline. For example, the population of New York expanded by 0.4 million between 1970 and 1975 through natural increase but, as a consequence of net out-migration of 0.6 million, the population fell. Net in-migration, however, added population to states in the South that were expanding through natural increase at well above average rates, thereby compounding the rate of growth. Thus Georgia gained 0.3 million between 1970 and 1975: 0.2 million through natural increase and 0.1 million through in-migration. Differences exist between states east of the Mississippi in the number of migrants gained and lost, but the overall picture is clear. A fundamental shift in the direction and volume of internal migration is creating a new regional distribution of population in the East.

In contrast, post-war trends in migration have worked progressively to the benefit of the Gulf, South-West, and Pacific states. This area has always been a net recipient of migrants and includes states in which in-movement constitutes the major component in population increase. For example, the 1970–5 growth in Florida was 0.1 million through natural increase but 1.3 million through net

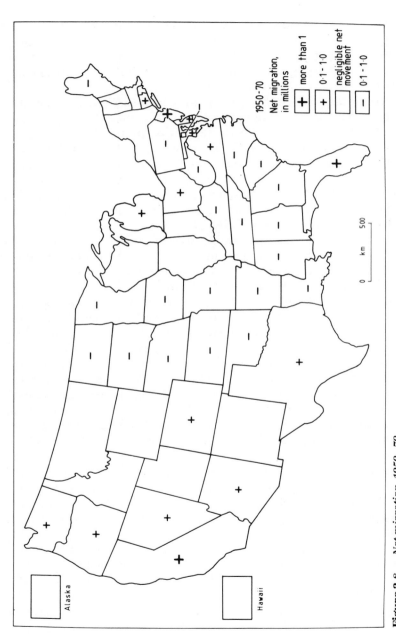

Figure 2.8   *Net migration, 1950–70*

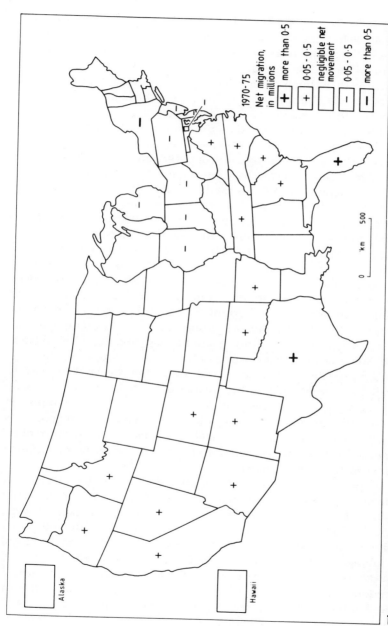

Figure 2.9   *Net migration, 1970–5*

migration. The figures for Arizona were 0.1 million and 0.3 million respectively. Generalization is difficult, however, because of the very different characteristics of states in the group, and suggestions that in-migration is the only factor involved are simplistic and misleading. Growth through natural increase is also very important as the example of California's 0.7 million gain through this source, as opposed to 0.3 million gain through migration, shows.

Closer inspection of the data reveals that migrational flows have ethnic characteristics that represent important additional dimensions in the changing geography of population in the United States. Between 1960 and 1970, the eight manufacturing belt states had a net out-migration of Whites totaling 1.2 million; however this was offset by a net in-migration of 0.9 million Blacks. In the five-year period 1970–5, the net out-migration of Whites was 1.8 million, a third more than in the whole of the preceding decade, while net in-migration of Blacks was 0.05 million. The main reason for the much reduced net in-migration of Blacks is that increasing numbers of Blacks are moving from the North to the South. As this is precisely the opposite direction to the traditional South to North movement, it has been termed "Black counterstream migration" (Johnson and Brunn, 1980). Two distinctive groups are moving South, each for different reasons. The return migrants include older, blue-collared, widowed, and divorced people who are returning home because the social climate has improved since the 1960s. The new or primary migrants are young, highly educated, and white collar; they perceive the race relations and quality of life to have improved sufficiently to merit a move. Black counterstream migration is comparatively insignificant in national terms but is indicative of an emerging trend which could well change further the ethnic balance between North and South.

Despite the fall in net in-migration by Blacks, the differential effects of growth through natural increase point to a continuing shift in the racial composition of the northern population. Already, one-third of all Blacks live in the eight manufacturing belt states where they are especially concentrated in the major cities. Washington (70 per cent), Gary (Indiana) (70 per cent), Detroit (63 per cent), Newark (58 per cent), and Baltimore (55 per cent) are all predominantly Black cities, and there are several smaller cities in the manufacturing belt where the Black population is in excess of 40 per cent and rising rapidly. Conversely, in the South, net in-migration of whites is redressing previous imbalances thereby evening out the racial mix. These differences in movement patterns between Whites and Blacks mean that social and cultural factors must be considered alongside jobs and environment in explanations of the changing distribution of population.

Local changes

Equally far-reaching shifts in the distribution of population are taking place at the local level. Up to 1970, metropolitan areas were expanding rapidly on a scale sufficient to create and maintain Gottmann's Megalopolis on the North-Eastern Seaboard (Gottmann, 1961) and to foreshadow the emergence of similar sized clusters between Chicago and Pittsburgh, and San Francisco–San Diego (Kahn and Weiner, 1967). Indeed Doxiadis (1966), extrapolating the then current trends in population growth and distribution, envisaged no less than twelve super-megalopolises in the United States by 2060. Since 1970, however, the pace of metropolitan growth has slackened appreciably, and non-metropolitan areas have expanded more rapidly. As at the regional scale, population mobility rather than the differential rates of natural increase is the key factor; net movement out of cities has in fact replaced rural out-migration as the dominant direction of flow. For Sternlieb and Hughes (1975) this change amounts to a developing metropolitan–non-metropolitan dynamic. Declining cities and expanding rural areas, together with southern and western shifts at the regional level, dominate the emerging population geography of post-industrial America.

The overriding feature of the distribution of people at the local level is their concentration in the nation's metropolitan areas. The original 168 Standard Metropolitan Statistical Areas (SMSAs), delineated in 1950, covered about 7 per cent of the total land area and contained 56 per cent of the population. In 1980, 169 million, that is 75 per cent of the population, lived on 11 per cent of the land area in the 318 SMSAs that were then defined. The general concept of the metropolitan area is one of a large population nucleus together with those adjacent communities with which the nucleus has a high degree of social and economic independence. Thus the 1980 standard provides that each SMSA must include at least:

(i) one city with 50,000 or more inhabitants, or

(ii) a Census Bureau defined urbanized area of at least

50,000 inhabitants and a total SMSA population of at least 100,000 (75,000 in New England), together with

(iii)   the county or counties in which the central city is located, and adjacent counties, if any, so long as they have at least 50 per cent of their population in the urbanised area, and

(iv)   "outlying counties" which are included if they meet specified requirements of commuting to the central counties and are of metropolitan character.

As the basic building block in most states (outside New England) is the county, the core covers a far wider area than the Central Business District, as the example of Detroit shows (Figure 2.10). Ignoring the daily urban system boundary which is a refinement suggested by Doxiadis (1969), the Census Bureau definition introduces a threefold distinction between central cities and suburbs (both within the SMSA) and non-metropolitan areas. On this basis, the United States population emerges as predominantly suburban: 45 per cent live in the suburbs; 30 per cent are central city dwellers.

The dominant trend in the redistribution of population at the local level is, however, deconcentration, both as a consequence of suburbanization and counter-urbanization. Shifts are taking place within SMSAs which mean that central cities house a decreasing share of the population. Similarly, non-metropolitan areas are growing more rapidly than metropolitan areas, thereby pointing to a revival in the fortunes of rural America. Analysis of trends at this scale is complicated by the fact that the number of SMSAs was increased from 243 to 318 between 1970 and 1980, but by comparing the redistribution of population during the 1960s with that during the 1970s, the basic trend becomes clear. Between 1960 and 1970, suburban areas outside the central city gained 16 million people, whereas the central cities and the non-metropolitan areas, which each gained around 4 million people, grew only modestly (Table 2.4). But during the 1970s, city centers failed to grow at all, and although the suburbs recorded significant increases, it was in the non-metropolitan areas that the greatest change occurred. Even based upon the new SMSAs, non-metropolitan America gained 7.5 million people and grew by 15 per cent over the period.

The stagnation and in many cases the absolute decline of central areas after so many decades of growth represents a profound and symbolic change in the population geography of the United States. It means that the areas which are now declining most rapidly are

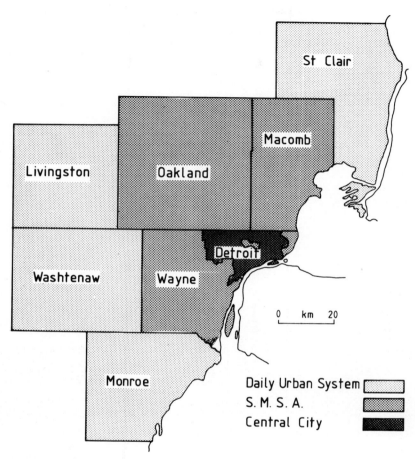

Figure 2.10   *Detroit Standard Metropolitan Statistical Area*

precisely those locations which were most sought after during the nineteenth and early twentieth centuries. As points of maximum accessibility they formed the pivots of urban-industrial economy and society. Today, as Berry (1975) has observed, they have become obsolete. Central area decline, suburbanization and non-metropolitan growth point to the progressive outward shift in the center of gravity of population at the urban scale. The movement of people within the city, from center to suburbs, is a long-established

Table 2.4 *Population by metropolitan and non-metropolitan residence, 1960–80*

	243 SMSAs				318 SMSAs			
	1960 *millions*	1970 *millions*	Change, 1960–70 *millions*	*%*	1970 *millions*	1980 *millions*	Change, 1970–80 *millions*	*%*
SMSAs, total	119.6	139.4	19.8	16.6	153.7	169.4	15.7	10.2
Central cities	60.0	63.8	3.8	6.5	67.9	67.9	0.0	0.0
Outside central cities	59.6	75.6	16.0	26.8	85.8	101.5	15.7	18.2
Non-metropolitan areas	59.7	63.8	4.1	6.8	49.6	57.1	7.5	15.1

Source: Statistical Abstract of the United States 1981, Table 19.

process which has created successive rings of development around the central cities over the past half century. It received a major impetus in the immediate post-war period when a combination of improved access to the center, via the newly constructed express-ways, and more readily available housing finance led to large-scale suburban developments in many United States cities. In 1950, 24 per cent of the population lived in the suburbs, but by 1960, this had risen to 33 per cent, and by 1970, 38 per cent (Muller, 1980).

In contrast, non-metropolitan growth is a far more recent and as yet poorly documented phenomenon. Berry's (1976) analysis suggests that approximately half of the new non-metropolitan growth between 1960 and 1970 was adjacent to metropolitan areas and so reflected no more than the spillover of population across an excessively tightly drawn SMSA boundary. A roughly equal portion of non-metropolitan growth was, however, non-adjacent to, and remote from, existing cities and so represented true non-metropolitan growth. The detail is provided by an analysis of the changing metropolitan structure of northern Ohio between 1960 and 1970 (Berry and Gillard, 1976). Maps of commuting to central Cleveland and central Akron in the two years both identified exurban residential developments arising as a result of workers moving further afield, seeking out new lifestyles in "rural" areas, and cutting their ties to the older central cities. The increased independence from the central area meant that the city had effectively declined in importance as an agent of spatial organization. "Thus what had previously been the intermetropolitan periphery was now displaying newly found independence as one of the region's new growth centers" (Berry, 1976, p. 23). During the period, metropolitan regions in northern Ohio became more dispersed. As older central cities declined, decentralization proceeded apace, metropolitan regions were restructured internally, and more amenity-rich outlying areas were brought into daily interaction with other parts of metropolitan America by changes in accessibility which were related to the construction of highways and expressways. Rather than more megalopolises, these trends point to the emergence of a dispersed urban society which will be lacking in what we today would recognize as major cities.

As at the regional level, migration, rather than the effects of natural increase, provides the key to the understanding of trends in population redistribution within and around cities. The most important feature of the last decade is the reversal of the long-established process whereby rural out-migration fed metropolitan growth. For many decades, rural people have moved into the cities, but between 1970 and 1980, SMSAs lost about 4.0 million people through net out-migration. For the first time this century, rural America grew at the expense of the city. Movement within SMSAs also had a pronounced directional bias as central cities lost about 9.0 million through net out-migration to the suburbs. Central cities in fact lost population to both the suburbs and to the non-metropolitan areas. The magnitude of these local shifts is rather less than that of movements at the regional scale but the direction and implications are the same. North-Eastern and urban America are deconcentrating to the South and West and to rural areas on the fringes of, and outside, the city.

Reasons for change

A great many factors are responsible for the emerging population geography of post-industrial America and, although some will be explored in detail in subsequent chapters, it is useful to outline the general reasons for change. The fact that the shifts are closely related to migration mean that the causes are much to do with space preferences; with changes in the values which people assign to different locations as places to live and work. As wealth and incomes have for most Americans long since passed the levels necessary for basic subsistence, so quality-of-life considerations have replaced economic necessity as primary determinants of location. Increasing numbers now aspire towards superior climate, space, lack of pollution and congestion, and access to unspoiled natural environment as the ideal. For Ullman (1954) this combination of attractions defines a new frontier, a frontier of comfort that contrasts with the frontier of hardship that is traditionally associated with the rigors of nothern manufacturing and, as Turner (1894) described, Great Plains settlement. Pleasant living conditions have superseded more narrowly defined economic advantages as primary spurs to movement.

Among the most important attractions at the regional scale is the pull exerted by climate. For Ullman (1954) the ideal climate, consisting of relatively mild winters and cool summers, low rainfall and abundant sunshine is to be found in southern California, the

Figure 2.11   *The sunbelt: mean air temperatures, °C, January*

protected coastal area of central and northern California, and the lower east coast of Florida. Almost as appealing are the climates which occur along the Gulf and South Atlantic coastal strips, in parts of the desert South-West, the Pacific coast, and the Colorado Piedmont. Distributions of temperature, precipitation, and sunshine hours do not coincide sufficiently to enable the popular conception of the sunbelt to be given precise geographical definition, indeed it is necessarily a somewhat vague notion (Browning and Gessler, 1979; Weinstein and Firestine, 1978) but the basic climatic contrasts between North and South are clear (Figure 2.11). The difference is most apparent in winter when the snowbelt states are contending with low temperatures, severe windchill, and blizzards, while Phoenix, Miami, Los Angeles, and San Diego bask in warmth and sunshine. Amenity is highest when favorable climate coincides with coast, mountain, or forest, this combination existing in a number of locations on the western and southern "rimland" (Berry, 1975). These areas offer a range of unspoiled environments which, paradoxically, because they were historically least valued and so left undeveloped, are today most highly prized (Berry, 1970). A general feature of the sunbelt south is the availability of cheap land, and lower building and maintenance costs (Estall, 1980). Although air conditioning is an additional expense, it is more than offset by lower winter heating bills. It has moreover made the humid South-East a more attractive area for permanent, year-round settlement.

Contributing to inter-regional and local migration from the opposite direction are a set of "push" factors associated with the deteriorating physical and social environment of manufacturing belt states and central cities. Whereas such areas were once seen favorably as places of economic and social opportunity offering jobs, good quality housing, and attractive urban lifestyles, their image today is of obsolescence, blight, dereliction, and decay. The contemporary association is with rising crime rates, acrimonious and violent confrontations, high levels of environmental pollution, rising taxes, poor schools, and declining city services. For those who could, the traditional response was to move to the suburbs, but abandoning the central city to low income and ethnic minorities served merely to exacerbate the problems and to stimulate additional and longer distance migration. Movement from the city altogether is seen by many as the logical reaction to the recent downturn in the fortunes of the nation's urban-industrial areas.

People are able to relocate in response to locational attractions, both real and perceived, because many of the traditional barriers to movement have been reduced or removed. The reasons are to do with the changing relationship between work and residence, and developments in transport and communications. One of the most far-reaching trends is the reduction in the importance of work as a locational constraint, both because of an increase in the number of people who are outside the labor force, and because many who are in employment have more flexible working patterns and indeed may work "remotely" from home. The elderly represent the largest and most rapidly expanding group of non-workers. As a consequence of improvements in diet, medical care, and health education, the population is living longer. Whereas the average life expectancy at birth for males in 1950 was 61, and for females was 65, the figures for 1980 were 70 and 78 respectively. The result was that in 1980 there were 26 million Americans over 65 years of age. Only about one-quarter of the over-65s work and so the elderly include a large number of people who are unconstrained in their locational choices by considerations of employment. Moreover, many of the elderly are comparatively well-off on account of a lifetime's earnings and capital accumulation, and so they can readily respond to their locational preferences. As a group, the elderly are highly attracted to areas of superior environment, both locally, and across the nation, in which to spend a carefree and relaxed old age.

Movement of population to areas of superior climate for medical reasons has been going on since the late nineteenth century, such that a "health arcadia" and a "sanatorium belt" have long been recognized in the South-West (Vance, 1972). Similarly, retirement migration, largely in response to climate, into Florida, south-western Arizona, and southern California, is a well-documented contemporary phenomenon (Golant, 1975, 1980). In 1980, over 17 per cent of the population of Florida was over 65. Within these sunbelt areas, many of the elderly live in purpose-built "retirement enclaves." Whole communities have been constructed with houses designed to save the elderly from exertion, with "roads, shops, banks, and churches built for the use of the car, and with recreational and learning facilities that will exhilarate but not tire, and with that careful balance between beauty and efficiency that will both inspire and satisfy" (Watson, 1979, p. 216). In consequence, many of the cities of the sunbelt, and in particular, Phoenix, Tuscon, St Petersburg, Fort Lauderdale, and Tampa, have very "top-heavy" demographic profiles because of their large number of elderly residents.

An increase in locational flexibility has also been extended to many people in employment on account of the changing nature of work and working practices. In general, the progressive reduction in the length of the average working week, which fell by four hours, or 10 per cent between 1960 and 1980, freed workers from the need to live close to work, thereby extending commuting fields deeper into non-metropolitan areas. A more specific, and a more recent, trend is the employment in computer and telecommunications based work which can be performed "remotely" without the need for the employee to visit the factory or the office every working day. Much has been written about the possible impact of telecommunications upon the distribution of population, and although the most extreme prognostications, that they will lead to a total dissipation of existing population clusters, can be dismissed as being fanciful, it seems clear that they will reinforce deconcentration (Clark, 1979).

Developments in transport and communication have also facilitated movement and migration at the national scale. Post-industrial technology has eroded the barriers of distance, time, and cost, thereby extending freedom of locational choice to an ever-increasing number of firms and individuals. Successive innovations in transportation have effectively shrunk the map of America as Janelle (1969) has shown, such that residence in the South and West no longer precludes regular visits to relatives and friends in the North-East. Few pairs of places in the conterminous United States are more than five hours' flying time apart, and the cost of air travel has fallen sharply in real terms since 1950. Similarly, telecommunications has replaced physical proximity by electronic proximity, enabling people to keep in touch irrespective of distance, and at low cost. Time-space and cost-space have indeed merged, as Abler (1975) has shown. These innovations have profound implications for the location of population, and for the distribution of industry as Chapter 3 shows. What exists increasingly in the United States is a uniform and low-cost accessibility surface across the continent within which individuals, both the elderly and those of working age, select to live and to locate their businesses in accordance with their perceptions of the social and physical environment.

For Berry (1975) the post-1970 developments, which are leading to an inversion in the population geography of the United States, are not to be interpreted as radical departures from established trends. Instead they are the products of very long-term and deep-seated processes in American society which have recently begun to bring about distributional changes at the national scale. Drawing upon de Crevècoeur's analysis of two centuries ago (Crevècoeur, 1782), he identified a variety of social and cultural traits, peculiar to the American character, which underlie the contemporary shifts of population. Thus a "love of newness" and an overwhelming "desire to be near nature" combine with "freedom to move" as primary factors in migration. They mean that Americans readily discard old and obsolete areas in their keenness to move to new natural environments. Indeed it is by means of movement, to achieve the goals of a superior lifestyle, that a "sense of destiny" is pursued. The migrational dynamic is reinforced by the operation of "the melting pot" through which social conformity and a continual reassertion of values is achieved. Though commonly associated with "violence," the fight to succeed skims off the upwardly mobile from a variety of backgrounds into the achievement-oriented mainstream of American society. Constraints which might otherwise inhibit rejection of the old in favor of the new are less powerful and restrictive in the United States because of the tradition of "individualism" which recognizes the right of everyone to choose and make decisions by reference to his or her own best interests. Berry's argument is that these cultural characteristics define a set of entrenched values which are directed firmly against the old urban–industrial areas. The traits which were previously responsbile for creating the manufacturing heartland with its industrial cities are now contributing to diffusion and deconcentration on both national and local scales.

Conclusion

This analysis of population growth and distribution has highlighted the basic demographic correlates of the emergence of the post-industrial society. At mid-century, national, urban, and North-Eastern populations were growing steadily, maintaining and reinforcing the regional, urban-rural, and central city-suburban differentials that had been established under high mass-consumption industrialism. Internal migration was strongly North-Eastern and urban centered, although particular localities in the Southern and South-Western periphery benefited from age-selected and income-selected movements. Today, national population growth is minimal on account of the very low birth rate. The manufacturing belt and its constituent cities are in stagnation or decline, while sunbelt states and cities are expanding rapidly. Deconcentration processes at the local scale point to the demise of central cities, and the revival of rural areas. The United States is turning itself upside down and inside out, with the population that was concentrated in the North-East and in city centers increasingly to be found in southern, western and rural areas.

These trends and patterns are products of the complex set of norms, aspirations, and expectations that comprise the value system of post-industrial society. Of central importance are the changes of attitude towards marriage and the family, in part reflecting the increasing range and attraction of alternative lifestyles, which result in women wanting fewer children. Restriction of family size is possible by use of advanced forms of contraception, most noticeably the pill, which ranks as one of the most important products of post-industrial technology. The geographical shifts of population result from changing attitudes towards space and location. These involve an increased attraction to high amenity environments, and a wholesale rejection of old and decaying areas, both locally and across the nation. Movements of people, however, constitute merely one component in the emerging geography of post-industrial America. Trends in the distribution of population are closely related in both a causal and consequential manner to the relocation of industry and employment.

3

Emerging patterns of industry and employment

Implicit in the concept of the post-industrial society is the replacement of goods production by service provision as the major focus of economic acitivity. The change involves the relative decline of manufacturing industry as a source of employment, and the rise to pre-eminence of the tertiary and, more especially, the quaternary and the quinary sectors. This general structural shift encompasses many complex changes involving the births, movements, and closures of firms, plants, and offices. Geographical consequences arise both because economic activities close in some areas and move elsewhere, and as a result of the differential growth of industry in cities and regions across the nation. Such absolute and relative changes in the location of economic activity alter the spatial distribution of both industry and employment. Together they create the economic geography of post-industrial America.

The most noticeable feature of the contemporary economy is the subordinate position occupied by the secondary sector. In contrast to mid-century industrial America, with its emphasis upon coal, oil, and steel, placebound extractive and heavy industries today account for a comparatively small percentage of the workforce (Table 1.2). The majority of Americans are employed in service

Table 3.1   *Employees in non-agricultural establishments, 1980*

Industry	Total employment (000s)
Mining	1020
Construction	4399
Manufacturing	20,300
Durable goods	12,181
Non-durable goods	8118
Transport and public utilities	5143
Wholesale and retail trade	20,386
Finance, insurance, real estate	5186
Services	17,901
Government	16,247

Source: Statistical Abstract of the United States 1981, Table 669.

production. A classification based on employment in non-agricultural establishments shows that manufacturing, and wholesaling and retailing establishments employ similar numbers (Table 3.1). As many people sell goods over the counter in wholesaling warehouses, shops, stores, restaurants, bars, drive-ins, and take-aways, as are employed in factories, foundries, and workshops. Manufacturing in fact employs only slightly more people than work in services (a category which includes personal, business, and health services, and the motion picture industry), and federal, state, and local government employment. Both services and government in 1980 accounted for more jobs than did manufacturing in 1950. Employment statistics, whether by industry or by type of establishment, are by no means a perfect measure of economic activity since they take no account of levels of productivity or value added by industry. The picture they convey, however, is one of an economy that has moved substantially away from a manufacturing bias towards the service/information orientation that is characteristic of a post-industrial economy.

Within the goods-producing sector, differences in the performance of the major manufacturing activities point to the emergence of a new industrial structure. Many of the old industries which powered the rise of industrial America in the late nineteenth and early twentieth centuries have declined in the post-war period,

Table 3.2 *Manufacturing employment, 1950 and 1980*

Industry	Total employment (000s)		
	1950	1980	% change
Durable goods			
Lumber and wood products	860	690	−19
Funiture and fixtures	330	469	42
Stone, clay, and glass products	461	666	44
Primary metal industries	1166	1144	−2
Fabricated metal products	838	1609	92
Machinery except electrical	1296	2497	93
Electric and electronic equipment	788	2103	166
Transportation equipment	1347	1875	39
Instruments and related products	201	709	252
Non-durable goods			
Food and kindred products	1495	1780	19
Textile mill products	1241	853	−31
Clothing	1065	1266	18
Paper	466	694	48
Printing and publishing	858	1258	46
Chemicals	659	1107	67
Petroleum	287	197	−31
Rubber and plastics	237	731	208
Leather products	387	233	−39

Source: Statistical Abstract of the United States 1953, Table 240 and *1981*, Table 669.

being replaced by those making the products demanded by the post-mass-consumption, information-intensive service society. The general nature of these structural shifts is depicted in Table 3.2, which shows the relative decline of the lumber and wood, primary metals, food, drink, and tobacco, textiles and clothing, and petroleum and coal industries as sources of employment. Conversely, fabricated metal products, machinery, electrical and electronic equipment, instruments and related products, chemicals, and rubber and plastics registered significant gains. Within these sectors, a number of industry groups recorded especially impressive performances. Because of the rate of contemporary growth, several of today's product classes were not recognized in 1950, but data for the period 1970–80 show that the fastest expanding industries were electronic components (52 per cent), office and computing machines (49 per cent), and drugs (30 per cent). These industries are by no means major employers on the national scale as the mere 430,000 in the office and computing machinery sector emphasizes but, like the railroad and its supporting iron and steel industry in the 1880s, they define "leading sectors" in the contemporary economy. As growth and technological pace setters, their space preferences are especially indicative of emerging and future locational trends in the geography of post-industrial America.

As well as a very different industrial structure, changes have also taken place in some of the factors which are considered by entrepreneurs in deciding where to open, expand, relocate, contract, or close down their economic activities. Of critical importance at the national scale are the changes in transportation which have opened up many previously remote and inaccessible areas for economic development. Foremost among the improvements was the construction of the interstate highway system in the 1950s and 1960s, consisting of 45,000 miles of high speed, low transportation cost, limited access highway linking the major cities of the nation (Figure 3.1). Although built primarily for strategic purposes, the system has had far-reaching implications for the movement of goods and the location of industry. In particular, it has benefited those cities of the South and West that were previously poorly served by state highways. Improvements in domestic air services made possible by the introduction of jet aircraft in the 1950s have further increased the range of locations open to business people. They have brought the North-East, West, and South coast much closer together. Especially important is the growth of Denver, Dallas–Fort Worth, and Atlanta as major southern and western nodes in the air network, both reflecting and reinforcing their status as major regional centers in the urban system (Figure 3.2). The greatest convergence of time and space has been achieved via improvements in the telephone system as Abler (1975) has observed. The progressive reduction in call charge rates means that cost as well as time and distance barriers to interaction have been removed. Moreover, the telephone network represents the basic infrastructure with which computer terminals can be interconnected across the nation.

A second shift in regional differentials concerns the costs associated with the changing geography of energy production and

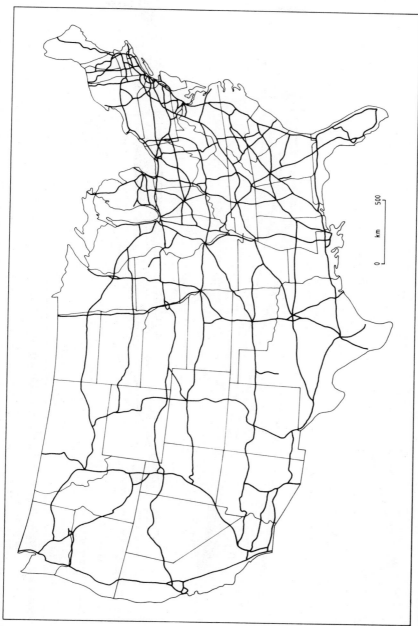

Figure 3.1 *The interstate highway network, 1981*

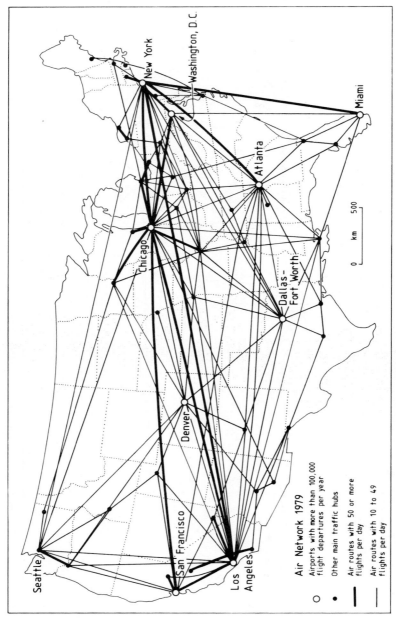

Figure 3.2   *Main elements in the domestic air network, 1979*
Source: *Watson (1982, p. 22).*

consumption. Since 1950, petroleum and natural gas have grown in importance at the expense of coal as an energy source (Table 3.3). At the same time, firms have become more energy conscious on account of the shortages and price rises which followed from the oil crisis associated with the 1973 Yom Kippur war in the Middle East.

Table 3.3 *United States energy sources: percentage uses, 1950 and 1980*

Fuel	1950	1980
Coal	38	21
Petroleum (oil)	40	45
Natural gas	18	27
Hydro-electricity	4	3
Nuclear electricity	0	4

Source: Statistical Abstract of the United States 1981, Table 991.

Table 3.4 *Crude petroleum, natural gas, and coal production by leading states, 1980*

Petroleum (million barrels)	
Texas	975
Alaska	592
Louisiana	467
California	357
Oklahoma	152
Wyoming	129
Natural gas (billion cubic feet)	
Texas	7169
Louisiana	6937
Oklahoma	1892
New Mexico	1142
Kansas	732
Coal (million short tons)	
Kentucky	150
West Virginia	112
Wyoming	95
Pennsylvania	87
Illinois	63

Source: Statistical Abstract of the United States 1981, Tables 1329 and 1332.

Together these trends serve to enhance the locational appeal of those states which are oil-rich and where energy requirements are low on account of climate. Such a coincidence occurs generally in the sunbelt and in particular in Texas, Louisiana, Oklahoma, and California (Table 3.4). The overall effects of energy are difficult to quantify in general terms because the distribution of fossil fuels both varies widely across the states and differs in terms of quality and value to industry. Moreover, costs to consumers may be equalized over large areas by producers, thereby eliminating advantages of location close to major energy sources. By totalling the heat equivalent of the oil, natural gas, and coal produced by each state and comparing it with the total heat consumed, Calzonetti (1980) has identified areas of energy deficit and surplus. His principal finding is that eight out of the ten leading energy-deficit states are in the traditional manufacturing belt. Nine of the eleven energy-surplus states are in the South and West in which Texas, Louisiana, New Mexico, and Oklahoma form a highly favored cluster.

The distribution of industry and employment

Although the four sectors of wholesaling and retailing, manufacturing, services, and government account for broadly similar amounts of employment, they differ markedly in terms of their distributional characteristics. These contrasts are shown in Figure 3.3 which uses location quotients to show the amount of employment in each sector in each state. Location quotients measure the degree to which an area has more or less than its share of any particular type of employment. The index is constructed by dividing the percentage of employment in a sector in a state by the percentage which represents that state's share of national employment. A value of 1.0 indicates that a state has exactly the amount of employment in a sector that its overall volume of employment would suggest. Values above 1.0 denote an over-representation of that sector, and values of less than 1.0 a deficiency. For example, Florida, with 4 per cent of the nation's overall employment has 2.3 per cent of all workers in manufacturing and 4.5 per cent of those in services and so has location quotients for these two sectors of 0.6

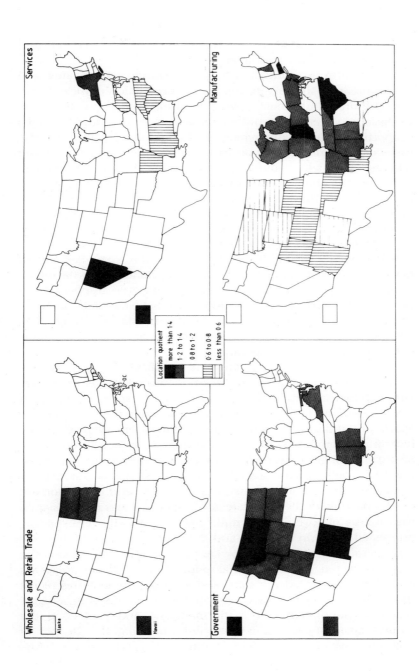

and 1.2 respectively. A common system of shading is used in Figure 3.3 so that the maps are directly comparable.

The uniform distribution of both wholesaling and retailing, and services reflects the very strong market orientation of these activities, and underlines their close relationship with population. Jobs in these two sectors are present in each state in nearly the same proportion as total employment and consequently there are few cases of concentration or under-representation. Wholesaling and retailing are highly ubiquitous and, other than the District of Columbia, the only examples of significant specialization in services are Nevada and Hawaii. Both are states with small base populations in which an orientation towards recreational and entertainment provision results in a far greater than expected share of service employment. Conversely, several states in the Old South have a deficient service sector. That the states of the North-East which have recently lost population do not also stand out as having an excess of employment in these sectors, however, testifies to the mobility of wholesale, retail, and service activities. Jobs in these sectors have migrated along with movements of people. The geography of wholesaling, retailing, and servicing is synonymous with the geography of population.

In common with wholesaling and retailing, and services, the distribution of jobs in government is relatively evenly spread, although there is over-representation in certain states. Government employment nationally includes 2.9 million who work for the legislature, judiciary, executive, and independent agencies of the federal government. Nine and a half million are employed by the 80,000 units of local government, including counties, municipalities, townships and towns, school districts, and special districts as recognized by the 1977 census of government, and 3.7 million are on the payrolls of the fifty state governments. Areas with a significant excess of government employment are mostly very sparsely populated states in the West and Prairies which have little in the way of manufacturing activity. Levels of employment above the levels expected given the total population in these areas are recorded for both federal, state, and local government and reflect the higher manpower needs associated with administering a highly scattered population, and with managing and protecting the natural environment. Otherwise, and excluding the District of Columbia, which with its concentration of government employment has the highest location quotient of any state for any activity, there is little evidence that public sector employment discriminates for or against particular states. Most government jobs are in state and local government and so their distribution across the nation closely reflects that of population.

In contrast to this comparatively even spread, there are pronounced geographical variations in the distribution of jobs in manufacturing. The range of location quotients is indeed widest for manufacturing, varying from 0.29 for North Dakota to 1.54 for North Carolina, the state with the greatest excess of jobs in goods production. In part, Figure 3.3 reaffirms a familiar dimension in the economic geography of the United States. Manufacturing employment is over-represented in a group of states in the North-East stretching from Illinois to New Jersey in the area which comprises the traditional industrial heartland of the nation. Conversely, it is deficient over an extensive part of the High Plains and Mountain regions. Indeed despite recent population expansion and economic growth in California and the South-West, no state west of the Mississippi exhibits any marked degree of specialization in manufacturing. What is distinctive about the contemporary distribution, however, is the existence of a new manufacturing belt in the Old South. Tennessee, Alabama, Mississippi, Arkansas, and the Carolinas all have location quotients above 1.2 indicating that they have a higher level of employment in manufacturing than would be expected given the size of their employment base. North and South Carolina in fact have a greater excess of employment in manufacturing than any of the other states. Two and a half million people are employed in goods production in these six southern states and, although this is only equivalent to the manufacturing labor force of Pennsylvania and Ohio, it represents a sizable proportion of total employment in the South. Relative to local employment, manufacturing is as important an economic activity in parts of the South as it is in the traditional industrial belt of the North-East.

Southern manufacturing for many years served primarily local needs. It involved the production of a wide range of goods for consumption within the region, and the scale of operation was consequently insufficient to form the basis of indigenous industrial growth. Such industries which served a wider market were those which processed the products of southern agriculture and resources. These included the manufacture of textiles and clothing; of wood, wood products, pulp and paper, and furniture; of tobacco products; and of petrochemicals. One consequence of this pattern was that the South had a poor industrial mix, lacking the primary manufacturing activities which were present in the prosperous North. The other was that much of southern manufacturing industry was low wage. This indeed was a major reason for the success of the textile industry which moved from New England during the immediate post-war period to take account of lower labor costs (Perloff *et al.*, 1960).

The emergence of the South as a major area of manufacturing reflects both the continuation and in some cases the revival of established industries, together with the addition of new employment in high wage, high capital-intensive areas. Despite a decline in importance nationally, textile manufacturing retains its importance in the South in general, and was the leading product in terms of value added by manufacture in North and South Carolina and Georgia in 1977. The industry in these states is concentrated in a string of small cities stretching along the Carolina Piedmont from Lynchburg (Virginia) to Atlanta (Georgia), including Roanoke (Virginia), Spartanburg and Greenville (South Carolina) and Ashville and Winston-Salem in North Carolina (Figure 3.4). As well as textiles, both cotton and artificial fiber, the principal specialisms of the region are tobacco processing, for which Raleigh, Durham, and Winston-Salem are particularly noted, and industries based upon Appalachian forests, such as furniture making and the manufacture of paper and boarding. The textile industry was initially attracted to the area by cheap labor, cheap power, and the local availablilty of raw materials. Today, most of the cotton for the mills is shipped in from Texas and points west, but labor is still comparatively cheap. In fact at 211 dollars (as compared to the US figure of 289 dollars), average weekly earnings in North Carolina were in 1980 the lowest in the nation. The chemical industry in the South has benefited from an increased demand for chemical products, and the abundant natural gas, oil, salt, sulfur, and phosphates deposits have attracted high capital investment which sustains a fast growth and prosperous industry. The manufacture of chemicals is widely spread throughout the South and ranks among the top three industries by value added in the Carolinas, Florida, Kentucky, Tennessee, and Alabama.

To these traditional activities must be added the new industries

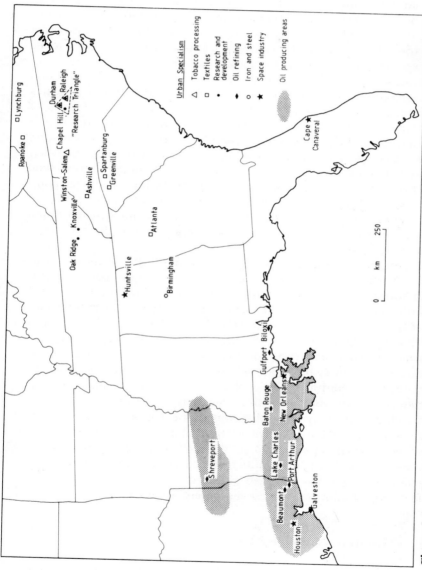

Figure 3.4 *Centers of manufacturing in the South*

which are responsible for the South's recent rise to importance as a manufacturing area. Foremost among these are industries supported by government contracts producing military and aerospace hardware and technology. The development of the space program especially in the 1960s caused billions of federal dollars to be expended in the South, especially in the "space triangle" with apexes at Houston (Texas), Huntsville (Alabama), and Cape Canaveral (Florida). This is turn spawned a wide range of activities in electronics and related fields (Norton and Rees, 1979). The role of science-based industry is further strengthened by the presence in the region of complexes of universities, laboratories, and research institutes, in the Carolina Piedmont "research triangle" between Raleigh and Durham, and at Knoxville/Oak Ridge (Tennessee). Although not as important in a national context as similar complexes in Boston, Palo Alto (California), and New York, the presence of significant levels of research and development finance in the area has been a significant factor in attracting new high technology industry to the South.

As a manufacturing region, the South has little in common with the North-East. Total employment in and concentration of manufacturing are less, and with the exception of the iron and steel industry of Birmingham (Alabama), there is an absence in the South of the large urban industrial complexes which give the northern industrial landscape its distinctive character. The types of industrial specialism also vary, and the presence of traditional resource and agriculturally based industries in the South remains strong. In part, these contrasts are explained by historical differences in natural wealth, but they also reflect the headstart in economic development enjoyed by the North. The lag is being overcome, however, through a revival of established industry and the addition of new. For Thompson (1975, p.188) "the South is going through the industrial and the post-industrial age at the same time." As a consequence, it has emerged as one of the major areas of manufacturing employment in contemporary America.

The manufacturing belt

Despite several decades of decline, the North-East remains the major manufacturing region. Wisconsin, Illinois, Indiana, Michigan,

Ohio, Pennsylvania, New York, New Jersey, and Connecticut together accounted for 8.7 million manufacturing jobs in 1980, 42 per cent of the national total, and produced 47 per cent of the value added by industry. It is indeed the total number of jobs in goods production rather than the ratio of those jobs relative to other sources of employment that accounts for the dominance of the manufacturing belt. Location quotients for manufacturing for the Northern states are no greater, and in some cases are smaller, than for states in the South.

As well as more manufacturing jobs in total, the North-East has both a different and a more diversified product base to that of the South. Metalworking and mechanical engineering are the most important and widespread activities in the area. Of the nine states in the North-East with location quotients in Figure 3.3 of over 1.2, four have primary metals industries among their three leading industry groups, and six specialize in the manufacture of fabricated metal products (cars, cutlery, tools, screws, forgings, etc.). Secondary working of metals to produce machinery (excluding electrical), that is engines and turbines, and agricultural, industrial, office, and domestic machinery, also figure prominently in six states as does the manufacture of transport equipment including motor vehicles, aircraft, ships, railroad equipment, bicycles and motorcycles, missiles and space vehicles (four states). Food processing, electrical equipment manufacture, and paper making are also significantly concentrated in the area.

It would be wrong, however, to infer from this list of diverse and varied products that the North-East is one continuous unbroken industrial belt, lacking in internal variation. This is neither the case today, nor was it true at mid-century. Although manufacturing is spread throughout the region, there are a number of points of concentration. Definition of such areas is necessarily arbitrary because it involves subjective decisions and so there is little agreement among analysts. It does, however, serve the useful purpose of drawing attention to the distributional character of manufacturing in the region. Ten major areas of specialization can usefully be distinguished in the manufacturing belt (Figure 3.5). Four are constituent parts of the Boston–Washington axis, while two are in interior Pennsylvania and New York. The remaining four are clusters of manufacturing in the eastern Mid-West. Each zone contains a contrasting mix of industries and manufacturing special-

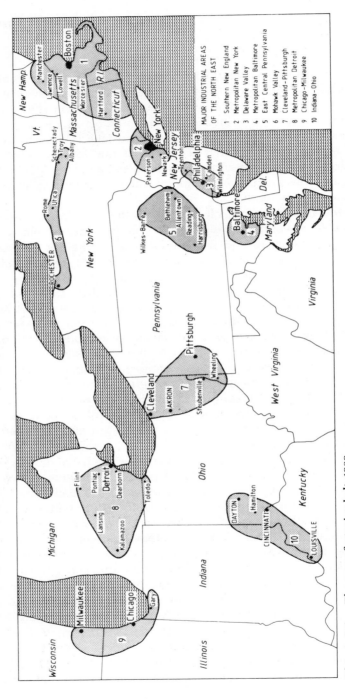

Figure 3.5 *The manufacturing belt, 1980*

MAJOR INDUSTRIAL AREAS
OF THE NORTH EAST

1 Southern New England
2 Metropolitan New York
3 Delaware Valley
4 Metropolitan Baltimore
5 East Central Pennsylvania
6 Mohawk Valley
7 Cleveland–Pittsburgh
8 Metropolitan Detroit
9 Chicago–Milwaukee
10 Indiana–Ohio

isms as a consequence of its differing historical and geographical circumstances.

In manufacturing terms, the Boston–Washington axis may be divided into four sub-regions: southern New England, metropolitan New York, the Delaware Valley, and metropolitan Baltimore. The southern New England area starts in the east with Greater Boston, extends west through Worcester and Springfield, runs down the Connecticut Valley past Hartford, and then moves south-west through New Haven and Bridgeport linking with the New York region. As a center of manufacturing industry, this is the oldest in the nation. Even before the Civil War, cotton production, based upon local water power, was well established, and for many decades the area led the United States in cotton and wool manu-facture and in the production of shoes and leather. The metals industry also developed comparatively early giving the region a wide-ranging but geographically dispersed industrial base. Although this early lead has long since been lost, the area remains a major center of manufacturing with an industrial mix that still reflects its historical roots. Among the dominant industries are textiles, leather goods, machinery (especially electrical), and cloth-ing. There is also a great variety of other types of manufactures such as jewelry, metals, shipbuilding, abrasives, paper products, rubber goods, and chemicals. The cotton textile industry was originally concentrated in south-eastern Massachusetts and Rhode Island. It reached its peak in New England just prior to the First World War when there were 18 million cotton spindles in the area (Alexander, 1975). But the last cotton weaving left Rhode Island in 1968, and most of the mills in the Greater Boston area are also gone. In some instances they have relocated in Maine where labor costs are cheaper, but for the most part they have moved south to the Carolina Piedmont. Woolen mills are concentrated in the Merrimack Valley cities of Lowell, Lawrence, and Manchester, to the north of Boston, as well as in northern Rhode Island. The decline has been less severe in the region than in the old cotton areas. Leather goods are another traditional industry of south-eastern New England, particularly in Boston, Brockton, Haverhill, and Lynn, although there has been considerable recent out-movement to the Mid-West and the South-East. Clothing has, however, retained its importance in the area in terms of value added, though with a much reduced employment due to the effects of automation.

The machinery industry is widely spread throughout southern New England. Greater Boston is especially important for textile and shoe machines, electrical products, and machine parts and tools. There are over 500 electrical machining plants in the Boston area alone, many of which are located along Route 128, the "electronics highway" where the research facilities of Harvard and the Massachusetts Institute of Technology contribute to the heavy concentration. Engineering remains strong in south-west New England both on account of the continuation of old established activities and the addition of new specialisms in the transportation equipment sector. Despite the movement away of much of the national market, the forces of inertia have kept most of the brass, hardware, typewriter, and machine tool industries in the area. All involve light manufacturing requiring few raw materials, little power, but advanced mechanical skill. The largest industry in south-western New England is United Aircraft of Hartford (Connec-. ticut), which manufactures aero engines at Pratt and Whitney, West Hartford, and helicopters at Sikorsky Aircraft in nearby Stratford. Otherwise, Connecticut lacks any dominant center, and machinery manufacture is scattered across a large number of small towns in common with the pattern of location of industry in New England generally.

In contrast, the overwhelming characteristic of the location of industry in metropolitan New York, the second area within the Boston-Washington axis, is its concentration. Half a million people are employed in 400,000 manufacturing establshments in the city and its environs, thus forming the greatest single cluster of productive capacity in the United States. A second characteristic is the variety of industry, as 90 per cent of the 500 types of manufacturing recognized by the United States Census are present in the metropolitan area. Clothing is by far the leading sector in New York City accounting for 140,000 employees in 1975, followed by printing and publishing (91,000), miscellaneous manufacturing (42,000), and food and related products (37,000). Heavy industries, while present in the region, are generally located outside New York City. Most are concentrated on the New Jersey shore in a cluster of old industrial centers including Jersey City, Newark, and Elizabeth, which have long been important for chemicals, petroleum refining, steelworking, machinery, shipbuilding and repairing, and food processing.

Port facilities are the greatest single reason for the concentration of industry in metropolitan New York. The Port Authority of New York and New Jersey handles about 40 per cent of the value of American foreign trade, or four times that of its nearest rival, New Orleans (Louisiana). New York City's magnificent harbor attracted shipping early, and the opening of the Erie Canal in 1825, linking New York via the Hudson and Mohawk with the lower Great Lakes, gave the city a headstart over its East Coast rivals for trade to and from the Mid-West. This in turn led to the growth of extensive wharves, warehousing and terminal facilities in adjacent New Jersey. As the geographical center of a highly populated hinterland, the port facilities of metropolitan New York became and remain the logical location for a wide range of processing, refining, and packaging activities.

Over the years, the influx of migrants, both internal and international, compounded urban growth and led to the development of market-oriented industries in the metropolitan area. Most industries in New York City are small scale and labor intensive and have traditionally benefited from the availability of unskilled immigrant workers willing to toil for long hours for low pay in order to establish a degree of financial security. Foremost in importance is clothing, an industry traditionally associated with large cities but notable in the case of New York City for its size and concentration. Between 25th and 40th Streets on Manhattan Island are several thousand workshops employing nearly a quarter of the nation's garment workers. Nearly half the concerns making women's clothing are located there. The recent attraction of new activities in the electronics and instrument sectors, combined with the spread of industry north to Westchester County and east to Suffolk County and Long Island, have given the metropolitan area both a more diviersified and a more dispersed industrial base than ever before.

Along the Delaware River, between Trenton (New Jersey) and Wilmington (Delaware), is the third major industrial complex in the manufacturing belt. Like metropolitan New York, the mix of industries is extremely wide, although the emphases are different. Heavy industry in the form of iron and steelmaking, shipbuilding and repairing, textiles, and chemicals manufacture predominates. The region is centered upon Philadelphia, America's fourth biggest city, which has textile, machinery and machine tools, high grade paper, food processing, transportation equipment, printing and publishing, and shoe and leather industries.

The area received a general stimulus to growth because of its tidewater position, and the Delaware River, which is navigable up to Trenton, remains the major locational attribute. Between Chester and Wilmington its western bank is lined with oil refineries and chemical plants, many of which are owned by the Du Pont Company. Shipyards predominate in Philadelphia, while at Morrisville (Pennsylvania), opposite Trenton, is the second largest of the East Coast steel mills, United States Steel's Fairless works. This plant, opened in 1952, employs 6000 and has an annual capacity of 4 million tons. It uses iron ore from Cuidad Bolivar in Venezuela, coal from Pennsylvania and West Virginia, and limestone from the Allentown area (Warren, 1973). Proximity to high-grade coal is the second advantage enjoyed by the region. One hundred miles to the north-east, between Reading, Scranton, and Wilkes-Barre is the only sizable anthracite field in the United States. The availability of coal is important in chemical manufacture and was responsible for the attraction of modern steelmaking to the lower Delaware Valley, although with the scale of recent contractions in mining in the area, East Pennsylvania is now insignificant as a coal producer.

A very similar complex of industries is located some 40 miles to the south of Philadelphia in the Baltimore metropolitan area. Although some 200 miles from Hampton Roads at the north of Chesapeake Bay, Baltimore is on tidewater and has a range of traditional processing industries including copper smelting, sugar and petroleum refining, and fertilizer manufacture that reflects its status as America's third most important port. There is also a wide diversity of secondary manufacturing industry including canning, textiles, clothing, and printing and publishing. Baltimore is, however, renowned as a steel city and Bethlehem Steel's Sparrows Point plant, built in 1887, is now the largest in the United States, with an annual capacity of 8.2 million tons. The plant uses iron ore from Venezuela, Chile, and other Latin American countries, coal from West Virginia, and limestone from Pennsylvania. It is also the leading point for the import of ore for transhipment to steel plants in the north-central United States. Baltimore is located towards the southern end of the 400-mile long Boston–Washington megalopolitan axis. Together, the four constituent industrial complexes of New England, metropolitan New York, the Delaware Valley, and metropolitan Baltimore, account for one-quarter of the manufacturing jobs and industrial establishments in the United States.

The rest of the manufacturing belt

In contrast to these areas of manufacturing concentration in Megalopolis, each of which developed around a major city, neither east-central Pennsylvania nor the Mohawk Valley industrial regions have a central urban core. Both contain a wide scatter of medium-sized urban areas together with several smaller cities. Over 1 million people live in the area bounded by Scranton, Wilkes-Barre, Allentown, and Bethlehem in an extensive region which, because of its dissection by the Blue Ridge of the Appalachians, has an element of economic but no physical unity. Conversely, the Mohawk River links a string of diverse manufacturing centers between Albany and Buffalo into a linear industrial region of some 3.5 million people. Industrial decline, however, is common to the two areas as shifts in population reduce the size of local markets and increase their relatively peripheral locations.

Manufacturing in east central Pennsylvania owes its origins to iron ores, which are still worked, in the vicinity of Bethlehem, limestone from Allentown, and coal from the Scranton–Wilkes Barre anthracite field. Steelmaking is long established in the area, and despite competition from tidewater mills, Bethlehem Steel's works in Bethlehem remains equal in capacity to the Fairless Plant (Warren, 1973). It supports a range of metalworking activities in the surrounding area. Though still centers of manufacturing, the anthracite towns of Scranton and Wilkes-Barre have lost much of their former importance. Textiles, clothing, silks, lace, shoes, and mining machinery are products manufactured in the area.

The cities of the Mohawk Valley, while benefiting in general from location along the line of easiest access from the East Coast to the Great Lakes, have varied manufacturing specialisms. With a mix of textiles, metals and machinery industries, they have much in common as regards employment structure with the towns of New England. Albany, Troy, and Schenectady together form an old industrial complex specializing in shirts and machinery, while Schenectady is the home of General Electric and American Loco-motive. Utica and Rome have a range of textile, carpet, metals, and machinery industries while Syracuse is a major producer of soda ash. Rochester on Lake Ontario produces cameras, electrical machinery, and optical equipment and is the home of Eastman Kodak and the Baush and Lomb electrical works.

If industrial diversity is the keynote of the Mohawk Valley towns, it is the importance of iron and steelmaking that gives the Pittsburgh–Cleveland area its distinctive character. The district includes the major steel centers of Youngstown and Wheeling–Steubenville as well as Pittsburgh and Cleveland, and accounts for 20 per cent of United States blast furnace capacity. Most plants in the area are owned by United States Steel, Jones and Laughlin, and Republic Steel. Many other types of manufacturing are also carried on including machinery and machine tools, tires and rubber products (especially in Akron, Ohio), clay products, and glass. Together with iron and steel these make the Pittsburgh–Cleveland area the leading heavy industrial center of the nation.

The iron and steel industries of the area developed because of the juxtaposition of local ores, now depleted, and Appalachian coal. They are sustained today by a complex set of movements of raw materials that varies according to season and to price. Iron ore is shipped into Cleveland and adjacent Lake Erie ports via the Great Lakes/St Lawrence Seaway system from both the Superior Uplands and from the Labrador–Ungava field in Canada. Some is moved by rail to Youngstown and Pittsburgh, but these cities also receive ores from Labrador and Venezuela which are transported by rail from the importing port of Baltimore. Coal from Pennsylvania and West Virginia mines moves to Pittsburgh by barge on the Monongahela River and to the other steelmaking centers by rail.

Despite the continuing availability of high grade coal in the Appalachians, the status of Pittsburgh as one of the nation's leading steel cities owes more to historical circumstance than to the contemporary economics of location. The site of Pittsburgh, at the point where the Monongahela and the Allegheny join to form the Ohio, gave it an early cost advantage in the assembly of raw materials so that the mills of the city were well placed to satisfy the demand for steel that was associated with the railroad boom of the post Civil War period. The translation of this locational asset into profit was achieved by Andrew Carnegie, who, by his bold application of the Bessemer process to steelmaking and by his financial expertise, dominated industry in Pittsburgh until he sold out to the newly created United States Steel Corporation in 1901. The power and vested interests of United States Steel is shown by its imposition of the "Pittsburgh Plus" pricing system. Under this arrangement, all steel sold in the United States was priced as if it had been made in Pittsburgh and shipped from there even though in reality the purchaser fetched it himself from his own local mill. It served to discourage the spread of production to outlying areas and to protect the high investment in steelmaking plant in Pittsburgh and the hegemony of the Corporation. Although declared illegal in 1924, it was replaced by a basing point pricing system which had similiar if less pronounced consequences. With the abolition of this system in 1948, the steel industry of the city was left open to unfettered competition. During the last thirty years, new steelworks have opened on the East Coast (at Morrisville) and elsewhere, and the dependence on foreign ores has increased. Pittsburgh remains a major center of iron and steel manufacture but occupies an increasingly peripheral location relative to the expanding markets of the South and West.

Industrial activities in the mid-western portion of the northern manufacturing belt are concentreated in Chicago, Milwaukee, metropolitan Detroit and in the Indiana–Ohio District. Chicago and Detroit have similar Lake Shore locations and so can be supplied with iron ore at relatively low transport cost from the Superior Uplands and, increasingly, Labrador. Coal is available from the Appalachian coalfields in Pennsylvania, West Virginia, and Kentucky, and from the interior coalfields in Illinois, Ohio, and Indiana. Metropolitan Chicago is in fact, with 31 million tons capacity, the nation's premier steelmaking center, and the miles of steel mills, petroleum refineries, and associated processing plants along the Lake Michigan shoreline between South Chicago and Gary (Indiana) represent one of the great concentrations of heavy industry in the world. As is to be expected of America's third biggest city, however, the range of manufacturing is diverse and includes electrical machinery, fabricated metals, food processing, printing, paper production, chemicals, and furniture. The array is extended by the industries of Milwaukee and surrounding towns which, reflecting their agricultural orientation, specialize in farm machinery and equipment, leather and leather products, meat packing and brewing. Together, these make the Chicago–Milwaukee district second only to metropolitan New York in terms of national manufacturing output.

The contemporary importance of metropolitan Chicago as a manufacturing center reflects the continuing influence of the transportation links to the continental interior that were so important to the city's historical development. Chicago first became established as the head of navigation for Lakes emigration routes to the West, but its industrial beginnings are related to the arrival of the first railroad from New York in 1852. In the last two decades of the nineteenth century, Chicago emerged as the hub of the American rail system, commanding a network of lines which linked the agricultural areas of the Mid-West and High Plains with the expanding urban markets of the East. The development of meat packing and food processing industries at the time reflected this intermediate position. The growth of heavy industry dates from the first decade of the present century and Chicago rose to prominence as a steel city on account of its exceptional transport links. The railroads were themselves major consumers of steel and the many lines radiating from the city enabled it to tap extensive markets for structural steel and metal products in the South and West. The twist in the spiral of urban growth added by the development of heavy industry increased the size of the population, so spawning a large number of market-oriented manufacturing activities. Despite its size and industrial complexity, however, Chicago remains a regional rather than a national city. It functions as the highest order distributive and administrative center for the Mid-West, a role which is reflected by its wide range of service industries.

Chicago is in this respect very different to Detroit which, as a single industry manufacturing city, has only limited servicing functions. Detroit is the most important of a number of centers in Michigan and adjacent parts of Ohio and Indiana, including Toledo, Flint, Lansing, and Kalamazoo, in which car, truck, and component part making overshadow all other activities. Unlike other cities in the United States, where there are merely vehicle assembly plants, the Detroit area is where engine blocks, bodies, suspension units, and trim components are both fabricated and assembled. For this reason, the automobile industry here is a major consumer of steel. Much is shipped in from Chicago, Pittsburgh, and Cleveland but there is significant production within the city. With 14 million tons annual capacity, principally from its River Rouge and Ecorse Plants, Detroit was, in 1972, America's third most important steelmaking city (Warren, 1973). As long as casting, forging, and body pressing remain in the city it is likely that Detroit will continue to dominate the United States automobile industry.

The final area of concentrated industrial activity in the manufacturing belt is the Miami Valley and central Ohio Valley in south-west Ohio, south-east Indiana, and adjacent parts of Kentucky. The Miami Valley produces a wide range of manufactured products including iron and steel, with blast furnaces at Middletown and New Miami, machine tools, aircraft, computers and calculators, cash registers, and a variety of other products that require skilled labor. The main centers of the Miami Valley are Dayton, the largest; Hamilton, with paper and paper making machinery a specialty; and Middletown with its steel mills and diversified industrial production. Metropolitan Cincinnati, with 1.4 million population in 1980, is the major city of the middle Ohio Valley and its early pork packing industries have been replaced by the development of a highly diversified manufacturing base that includes machine tools, automobile parts, electrical equipment, and aircraft engines. Downstream is Louisville (Kentucky), a city specializing in domestic appliance manufacture as well as in the more traditional industries of cigarette making, chemicals production, distilling, and furniture.

Taken together, these ten industrial regions account for most of the 8.7 million jobs in goods production that justify the continuing designation of the area between Chicago and New York as "manufacturing belt." However, they by no means exhaust the productive capacities of the region for there are many additional centers and districts scattered across the North-East and Mid-West that contribute on a smaller scale to the industry of the area. In particular, there are numerous towns in the Appalachian Valley in Pennsylvania that are heavily engaged in manufacture. A second qualification is that the major manufacturing districts as described here are not to be taken as definitive and precise units for, as was explained earlier, their delimitation is necessarily one for subjective judgment. Questions of areal extent and boundary drawing are always relative in regionalization. What they highlight, however, is the diversified industrial base of the area. What distinguishes the contemporary manufacturing belt is both the large scale and the wide range of its constituent industries.

Three further features characterize the northern manufacturing states. The first is that, despite the wide range of industries in general, parts of the belt are highly dependent upon particular sectors. The fortunes of Detroit remain closely bound up with those of the automobile industry, as do those of the Pittsburgh–Cleve-

land and south-western Pennsylvania areas with steel. The low level
of industrial diversification in these areas is not necessarily dis-
advantageous as long as these primary manufacturing sectors
remain buoyant, but if they enter recession there is little in the way
of alternative employment. A second feature is the historical
rationale but limited contemporary justification for the location of
industry in many parts of the belt. Minimum cost assembly of coal
and iron ore was the guiding locational principle for the siting of
basic heavy industry in the region, and present-day distributions
owe much to continuing inertial effects. Areas like south-west
Pennsylvania, Pittsburgh, and parts of New England, however, are
highly peripheral in terms of contemporary markets and offer little
in the way of locational appeal to high technology modern manufacturing. The third observation is that much of the industry in the
region is market-oriented. Demand is provided by the great concentrations of population that comprise the major metropolitan
centers of the North-Eastern Seaboard and the southern Great
Lakes. If these clusters dissipate, as current trends in the distribution of population suggest, then the basis for a wide range of
market-oriented industry will be undermined.

Industrial corporate control

The economic importance of the manufacturing belt stems not
merely from the type and range of its industries and the workforce
employed in them, but from the degree to which it exercises a controlling influence over American industry. Industrial production,
finance, banking, and insurance in the United States, as in most
other advanced economies, are dominated by a small number of
very powerful corporations, and it is from the head offices of these
companies that corporate empires spanning most of the states, and
in many cases large parts of the world, are organized and administered. The location of corporate decision making defines the major
points of economic power within the space economy. At the same
time, head office employment is important in itself, contributing
large numbers of highly paid white-collar jobs to the labor market
and bringing prestige and status to the local area.

The most important feature of the location of corporate head offices in the United States is their exceptional concentration in the North-East (Table 3.5). Of the 500 largest industrial corporations for which data are published in *Fortune* magazine, no less than 165 had head offices in the Middle Atlantic Division in 1975. A further 137 were controlled from head offices in the East North Central Division. Together, these industrial companies were responsible for two-thirds of the top 500's sales, assets, and employment. The remaining 198 of the top 500 corporations had head offices spread across the seven remaining Divisions covering forty-two states. Despite the South's contemporary importance as a manufacturing region, only 63, that is 12 per cent, of the top 500 industrials were controlled from head offices located in its three Divisions. This pattern of concentrated industrial decision making is broadly similar to that of the control centers of the United States banking and insurance industry (Daniels, 1975).

The major reason for this pattern is that head office functions are an urban activity. Corporate decision making relies for its effectiveness and success upon access to information, frequently of a random and uncontrolled nature, concerning the movement of stock markets, developments in technology, changes in government policy, fluctuations in exchange rates, and the economic health of suppliers and markets. For this reason, head offices are attracted to

Table 3.5 *Distribution of the 500 largest industrial corporations by division of headquarters location, 1955–75*

Census division	Corporate head offices 1975	Change 1955–75
New England	43	+21
Middle Atlantic	165	−53
East North Central	137	−14
West North Central	34	+ 4
South Atlantic	33	+10
East South Central	4	+ 2
West South Central	26	+12
Mountain	8	+ 4
Pacific	46	+14
Data not available	4	0

Source: Fortune, (1956, 1976).

the largest urban centers which have the widest range of firms, branches of government, finance capital institutions, and research laboratories. Control functions in the United States are, as a consequence, concentrated in the major cities of Megalopolis and on the southern Lake Shore. In 1975, seven out of the leading ten centers of industrial corporate control were in the manufacturing belt. The New York Metropolitan Area was the most important single center with head offices of 136 of the top 500 in the *Fortune* list. Of these, 98 were in the New York SMSA itself. Chicago (47), Los Angeles (23), Cleveland (20), Philadelphia (18), Pittsburgh (15), Detroit (14), San Francisco (13), Minneapolis–St Paul (13), and Boston (12) complete the list. As well as locational inertia, this distribution reflects the lack of major cosmopolitan cities outside the North-East and West Coast. Houston (11) and Dallas (6) were the only significant centers of corporate decision making in the South.

Research and development activity

As well as their manufacturing plants, co-ordinated through a hierarchy of offices from the corporate head office, the modern industrial firm typically has a specialized research and development (R & D) division. In early industrial America, product development was usually carried out alongside the production process by small firms, many of which, together with their innovations, failed to survive. Today, the R & D needed for new products has become a large and expensive process, involving long "lead" times between invention and production, and as such is beyond the scope of small firms with limited capital and expenditure. For Bell (1973), the growth of R & D is indeed one of the most important characteristics of the post-industrial economy, reflecting both the increased emphasis upon theoretical science, and the planned development of technology. The total R & D budget in the United States in 1969 was $69 billion, an increase in real terms of 300 per cent over the 1955 figure. Funding was provided almost equally by the federal government and by industry, the universities and other non-profit making institutions contributing only 4 per cent. Half of the federal R & D budget was devoted to defense, principally in the fields of aerospace, electrical systems, and electronics. In 1975 there were about 6000 industrial R & D laboratories in the United States, but 598 firms were responsible for some 95 per cent of R & D expenditure (Johnston, 1982).

The vast expenditure necessary for research into the development of new processes and products not only confines such work to large corporations, but also means that it is likely to take place in the major urban agglomerations where the relevant specialized information is available. R & D is like head office functions in that it requires strong links with external agencies, but in this case the organizations involved are firms, technological universities, and other research institutes. As a consequence, R & D is heavily concentrated in the major cities of the North-East, both reflecting and reinforcing the distribution of production, higher education, and corporate control (Figure 3.6). It is an especially important activity in the Boston–Lawrence–Lowell, Washington, Philadelphia–Wilmington–Trenton, Madison (Wisconsin), and Lafayette (Indiana) areas. Few centres of R & D work are, however, found outside the North-East, and only the San Francisco–Oakland–San Jose, Denver–Boulder, Austin, Huntsville (Alabama), and Raleigh–Durham (North Carolina) areas have a disproportionate concentration of both laboratories and research employees.

This pattern reflects the decisions of both the federal government and industry as to where to locate their R & D activities. Federal R & D is either undertaken in-house, in federal facilities, or is contracted out to industry, universities, and other non-profit organizations. R & D at federal facilities is restricted to a comparatively small number of centers of which Washington is by far the most important. Individual cities where there are major federal laboratories are also notable recipients of intramural R & D funds. These include the "space triangle" cities of Houston, Huntsville (Alabama), New Orleans, and Melbourne–Titusville–Cocoa Beach (Florida) (NASA); Oak Ridge–Knoxville (Tennessee) and Albuquerque (New Mexico) (energy); Pensacola (Florida) and Newport News–Hampton (Virginia) (defense); and Dayton (Ohio) (aerospace). As a consequence, federal intramural R & D is both far more geographically dispersed and city-specific than is R & D generally.

Universities and colleges performed about 12 per cent of all federal R & D in 1977, most of it in basic research (Malecki, 1980). Nearly one-third of this work was performed by the fifteen leading research universities which are concentrated in three areas. The

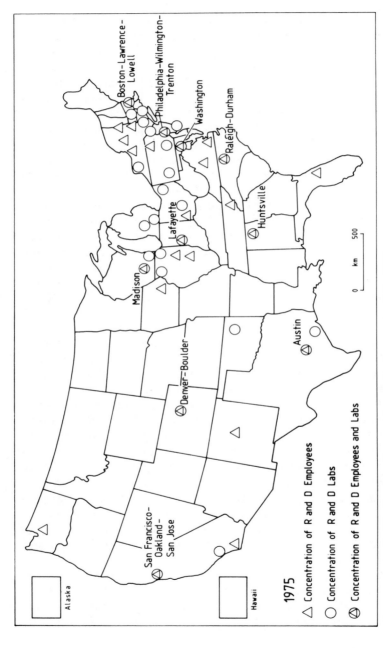

Figure 3.6 *The distribution of research and development activity, 1975*
Source: Malecki, E.J. (1979) "Agglomeration and intra-firm linkage in R & D location in the United States," Tijdschrift voor Economische en Sociale Geografie, 70, p. 328.

first is on the East Coast, including the Massachusetts Institute of Technology, Harvard, Columbia, Pennsylvania, Johns Hopkins, and Cornell. A second is the Mid-West including Michigan, Wisconsin–Madison, Minnesota, and Chicago, while the third concentration comprises the West Coast universities of Washington, Berkeley, Stanford, California–Los Angeles, and California–San Diego. The fact that metropolitan New York contains nine of the top one hundred research universities (including Columbia); Boston, 4 (including MIT and Harvard); Los Angeles, 3 (including UCLA) and San Francisco, 3 (including Berkeley and Stanford) means that these cities rank as major centers of university research. Outside the North-East, Mid-West, and West Coast there are few concentrations of university research, although Houston, and Raleigh–Durham (North Carolina), the latter with its "research triangle" universities of Duke, North Carolina–Chapel Hill, and North Carolina State, are notable exceptions.

In deciding where to locate its R & D laboratories, a firm attempts to equate the needs of the research process with the interests of the corporation as a whole. Ironically, what many corporate researchers (especially those in basic research) prefer is a noncorporate atmosphere, and for this reason, only eight of the fifty-eight cities which had more than five corporate laboratories (of the 330 largest US firms) in 1977 had both the primary R & D capability and the headquarters office of the same firm (Malecki, 1980). Almost half of all industrial R & D takes place in manufacturing cities where development work can be linked directly to production. As a consequence, particular centers specialize in particular types of R & D. For example, the Boston and San Francisco–Palo Alto (Silicon Valley) areas have marked concentrations of the laboratories of electronics firms; Los Angeles specializes in aerospace R & D; San Diego in biological and related pharmaceutical research; and the Philadelphia region in chemical R & D. The remaining industrial R & D activity takes place in university research centers and so is concentrated in the North-East, Mid-West, and West Coast. The combined effects of these locational considerations is, as shown in Figure 3.6, a distribution of R & D activity that at the national scale relates strongly to the distribution of population. Large metropolitan areas have the wide range of firms and productive specialisms, and the university-based expertise that provides the necessary links and stimulus for the R & D process. They also include within their labor

markets highly qualified and experienced research and technical
personnel. The pattern that results from the locational decisions of
both federal and industrial R & D managers and workers is a
concentration near large metropolitan centers where cultural and
recreational attractions are abundant, and especially at suburban

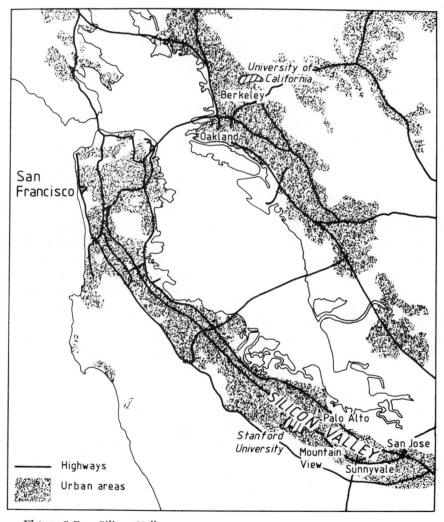

Figure 3.7   *Silicon Valley*

sites where home environment and schooling are acceptable to educated researchers.

One of the most important areas of concentrated R & D activity is in the Palo Alto–Santa Clara–San Jose area to the south of San Francisco Bay, a region known popularly as "Silicon Valley" (Figure 3.7). It was here that the silicon chip, the successor to the transistor and the basis for the microprocessor, was invented, and the Valley has become the leading R & D center for the United States computer industry. Although electronics components manufacture in the Valley traces its origins to 1938 when Hewlett-Packard began operations in a small garage shop in Palo Alto, the foundations for future growth were established by Nobel prizewinner William Shockley, a co-inventor of the transistor, who founded Shockley Transistor at Palo Alto in 1956. In moving into the Valley from the East Coast, he was attracted by the pleasant environment and the high standard of living that was possible amid the plum, pear, apricot, and cherry orchards of the southern Bay area (Johnston and O'Rear, 1982). Within a year, eight of Shockley's ablest collaborators left and, with the backing of Fairchild Camera and Instrument Corporation, set up Fairchild Semiconductors. Research at this firm undertaken by Robert Noyce, and exactly paralleling that by Jack Kilby at Texas Instruments in Dallas, was responsible for the invention of the silicon chip in 1958. During the next two decades, more than fifty new companies, including Advanced Micro Devices, Atari, Intel, and National Semiconductor were established in Silicon Valley by "Fairchildren," scientists who formerly worked for Fairchild. Their existence and success attracted further companies making photo-masks, testing jigs, chemicals, and silicon chips to the Valley, so that, between 1940 and 1980, total employment in Santa Clara County grew about 1000 per cent, from 60,000 to 652,000 (Saxenian, 1983). Although the manufacture of mainframe and minicomputers in the United States is dominated by IBM, Burroughs, Digital, and Prime, which are based elsewhere, Silicon Valley remains the major center of computer R & D, and of components manufacture. In 1970, five of the seven largest semiconductor firms in the United States had their main facilities in Silicon Valley, and clustered around them was the largest concentration of electronic communications, laser, microwave, computer, advanced instrument, and equipment manufacturers in the world (Saxenian, 1983).

The history of Silicon Valley underlines the reasons why centers of R & D develop and prosper. Cross-fertilization of ideas is essential to creative effort, and is most likely to occur when specialists are researching alongside each other. Similarly, competition between firms, reinforcing the drive to succeed, is keenest where R & D labs are adjacent. In initially promoting the area, a key role was played by Stanford University which established an industrial park in the early 1950s with the express aim of bridging the divide between higher education and industry. Leases in the park were granted only to high technology firms which were both beneficial to Stanford and which gained from the proximity of research facilities, expertise, and expenditure in the university. The park was also attractive in its own right as a location on account of its campus-style setting and pleasing landscape. Together, these locational attributes made the area a rich breeding ground for research and technology-intensive industry (Bylinsky, 1974). As such, it has become the most important national center for the new growth industries in the biotechnology sector (Feldman, 1983). Silicon chip and microprocessor research is by no means representative of all forms of R & D, but the emergence and success of Silicon Valley companies testify to the benefits of the mutually reinforcing competition that results from geographical concentration.

Changes in the location of manufacturing

Although the manufacturing belt remains the dominant feature of the industrial geography of the United States, its importance is diminishing in both absolute and relative terms. A pronounced regional shift is taking place which involves the decline of the North-East and the rise of the South and West. Similarily, at the local level, industry and employment are deconcentrating to the outer suburbs and beyond to the non-metropolitan areas. These trends at both national and local levels account for and reflect the changing distribution of population as outlined in Chapter 2. The processes of plant closures and movements involved are almost the exact opposite of those which created the distribution of economic activity at mid-century. As such, they are creating what for Sternlieb and Hughes (1978) amounts to a "new economic geography of America."

The general pattern of regional change is shown in Table 3.6 in which employment in non-agricultural establishments in 1960 and 1980 is disaggregated by Census Region and Division. Over this twenty-year period, the employment base of the United States increased by 67 per cent or 36.8 million jobs, but the growth was far from evenly distributed throughout the country. While the North-East recorded only a 31 per cent increase and the North Central Region, 50 per cent, rates of growth far below the national average, employment in the South and West more than doubled. Indeed though the South's total employment in 1960 at 14.2 million was below that of the North-East's 15.6 million and the North Central Region's 15.8 million, by 1980 it was the dominant employment locus in the country with 29 million jobs. Within the North-East, the Middle Atlantic Division, comprising New York, New Jersey, and Pennsylvania, did worst growing at a mere 26 per cent. Over this twenty-year period, the Division, which at mid-century comprised

Table 3.6   *Total employment change, 1960–80*[1]

| Region and division | Numbers in thousands | | | |
	1960	*1980*	*Change*	*%*
North-East	15,616	20,486	4870	31
New England	3704	5474	1770	48
Middle Atlantic	11,912	15,012	3100	26
North Central	15,837	23,730	7893	50
East North Central	11,643	16,827	5184	45
West North Central	4194	6903	2709	65
South	14,246	29,071	14,825	104
South Atlantic	7215	14,625	7410	103
East South Central	2760	5133	2373	85
West South Central	4271	9313	5042	118
West	8336	17,544	9208	110
Mountain	1872	4485	2613	140
Pacific	6464	13,059	6595	102
United States	54,035	90,831	36,796	67

Note: [1] Employees in non-agricultural establishments.

Source: Statistical Abstract of the United States 1971, Table 344, and *1981*, Table 668.

the heartland of the industrial economy, became the most laggard part of the United States.

These shifts in total employment are primarily products of the regional growth performance of the manufacturing sector. Over the twenty-year period 1960–80, manufacturing employment in the North-East declined at an accelerating rate, while in the North Central Region it rose significantly and then fell. In the South and West it grew continuously. As a consequence, the South in particular increased in importance as a region of manufacturing employment while the North stagnated. The detail is provided by a comparison of manufacturing employment in the 1960s with that in the 1970s. Between 1960 and 1970, manufacturing employment in the United States underwent significant growth, increasing by 2.7 million jobs or about 16 per cent of the 1960 figure. Regional performances, however, varied widely. Employment in the North-East remained essentially static whereas the North Central Region gained nearly 700,000 manufacturing jobs. The South did even better, increasing its manufacturing employment base by 1.5 million. In contrast, the decade of the 1970s was one of absolute decline in the North and further growth in the South. Although national manufacturing employment increased by 900,000 between 1970 and 1980, losses were recorded by the North-East and North Central Regions. The North-East alone declined by half a million manufacturing jobs while the previous gains of the North Central Region became losses of 170,000. Conversely, the South gained a further 900,000 manufacturing jobs over the period. These figures are not as large as those observed by Sternlieb and Hughes (1978) in the recession-hit mid-seventies but the overall trends are the same. They point to a recent but fundamental shift in the location of manufacturing activity, with the South identified as the emerging manufacturing core of post-industrial America.

Underlying these regional trends are a set of more detailed shifts in manufacturing employment at the states level (Figure 3.8). The most noticeable feature is the extensive area of absolute decline in manufacturing employment over the period 1970 to 1980. Every state in a continuous belt stretching from Connecticut to Delaware on the East Coast, and inland to Missouri, experienced an absolute reduction in the number of goods producers. Several of the states are extremely small and so the decline amounts to only a few thousand, but in others the magnitude of loss was substantial. New

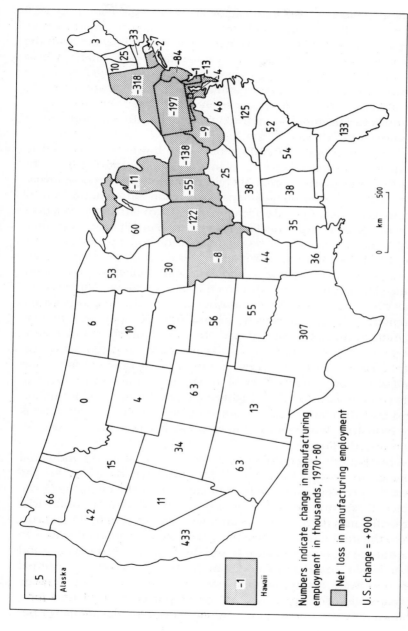

Figure 3.8 *Change in manufacturing employment, 1970–80*

York alone lost 318,000 manufacturing jobs, 18 per cent of its 1970 total, and Illinois, Ohio, and Pennsylvania each declined by over 100,000. Within the North-East, the states of New England, with the exception of Connecticut, did comparatively well. States which recorded the greatest gains were the highly populated states of Texas and California where manufacturing employment increased by 307,000 and 433,000 respectively. The consistent increase in manufacturing employment throughout the South is as noticeable a feature as the decline in the North.

These geographical trends should not, however, be viewed as evidence that manufacturing plants are simply moving from the North to the South. Industrial change is a complex process involving births, deaths, acquisitions, expansion and contraction of firms, as well as physical relocation, and so growth in one area does not necessarily imply decline in another. For Allaman and Birch (1975) more than half of the manufacturing employment losses in the North-East between 1970 and 1972 occurred because existing firms went out of business. Almost all the remaining losses were caused by existing firms reducing the size of their workforces. Only 2 per cent of job losses were attributable to out-migration of firms from the region. Conversely, in the South 65 per cent of new manufacturing jobs resulted from the expansion of existing plants, 34 per cent from completely new firms or branch plants setting up in the region, and only 1 per cent from in-migration of firms that had shut down plants elsewhere. The economic environment of the contemporary South is highly conducive to new firm formation and growth. The North, in marked contrast, holds few attractions for industrial developers and in consequence is an area of contraction and decline.

This pattern is confirmed in Rees' (1979) study of industrial change in Texas based upon 5839 locational decisions for the Dallas–Fort Worth and the Houston areas over the period 1960–75. Since these two areas are among the most dynamic industrial growth zones in the United States, Rees expected to find that firms from the traditional manufacturing belt had expanded into Texas to capture new sources of supply and new markets. Instead he found that locally based firms and new firms, as opposed to external sources, were responsible for most of the manufacturing growth. Expansions accounted for 2230 or 38 per cent of all decisions, followed by 2102 new plants (36 per cent), 790 relocations (14 per cent) and 717 acquisitions (12 per cent). Some important differences were noted between industrial sectors and between the two urban areas, but the overall picture is clear. Decline in the North-East does not automatically mean expansion in the South. The South is increasing in importance as a manufacturing region because it is both attractive to new firms and is an area which is conducive to industrial expansion and growth.

The reduction of manufacturing activity is paralleled by a decline in industrial corporate control in the North-East. Since 1955, a more dispersed pattern of the headquarters offices of the nation's top 500 industrial corporations has emerged (Semple, 1973; Rees, 1978). This deconcentration is indicated by significant gains of corporate head offices in the West, South Central, South Atlantic, Pacific, and New England Divisions, while the Middle Atlantic and East North Central regions show up as losers (Table 3.5). Gains in the West South Central Division were due primarily to the relative growth of the Dallas, Houston, and Tulsa metropolitan complexes. Data on the value of sales and assets, and number of workers on the payrolls of the "top 500," exhibit similar shifts to that of corporate head offices showing that a spatially less concentrated pattern of corporate control is emerging (Stephens and Holly, 1980). New York, Chicago, Philadelphia, and Detroit controlled a notably smaller share of the total assets of the "top 500" industrials in 1975 than in 1955. Conversely, Houston, Dallas–Forth Worth, Atlanta, and Los Angeles registered the most impressive gains in assets controlled.

As in the case of manufacturing employment, the factors underlying the redistribution of corporate control at the regional level are complex. A relocation element is involved, but it is not enough to suggest that corporate head offices are moving to the South and West because of the climate, recreational opportunities, taxation, or labor cost advantages. The most important reason for the shift is that a number of existing corporations in the aerospace, energy, telecommunications, and electronics industries, with headquarters in the South and West, grew sufficiently to enter the "top 500," displacing firms with headquarters in other regions. The fact that the corporate head offices of these expanded firms are concentrated in a small number of sunbelt cities enhanced the contact environment in those cities and attracted migrant head offices of other firms. The larger and more diverse the cities of the South and West become, and the greater their degree of national economic importance, the more corporate head offices from elsewhere they are likely to attract. While most corporate head offices remain tied to the nation's largest metropolitan areas, many have moved the comparatively short distance from the central area to the suburbs, or to locations within the wider metropolitan region. There they can maintain most of their established contacts which provide access to critical information, but can avoid the rent, service, and commuting costs of the central city. The most extreme example of concentrated dispersal is provided by New York in which the number of corporate head offices fell from 142 to 98 between 1955 and 1975 (Quante, 1975). Most moved to adjacent areas of Connecticut, such as Bridgeport–Stamford–Newark so in part explaining the rise of New England as an area of corporate control. Similar shifts within the urban area were recorded by Chicago, Detroit, Pittsburgh, and Philadelphia.

The decline in industry in the manufacturing belt, which began in the late 1960s, points to a fundamental reversal of the heartland-hinterland relationships which have traditionally underpinned the economic geography of the United States. Viewed from a spatial perspective, the United States economy consisted historically of a compact innovative core in the North-East and upper Mid-West, and an extensive adoptive periphery in the South and West. In performing its core functions, the manufacturing belt was the major center of innovation and change, acting as a seedbed for new ideas and innovations. New products were fabricated in the area throughout the early stages of the product cycle, but when the product became sufficiently standardized, manufacture was moved to branch plants in the periphery, both to maximize the cost advantages of localized production, and to enable the core to concentrate upon its successors. Until mid-century, the rate of repetitive innovation exceeded that of manufacturing loss, so the core retained its vitality and prosperity. Since 1970, however, it has fallen behind so that the core has been overtaken by the periphery. Although the reasons for the rise in innovative capacity in the South and West are many and varied, two elements were critical (Norton and Rees, 1979). One was the development of the Gulf Coast petrochemical industries and the stimulus this gave to scientific research in the area; the other was the role of "military-industrial contracts" that encouraged the avionics industry during the space race and Vietnam war years of the 1960s. The latter was not, however, the result of any explicit regional bias in the distribution of government procurement contracts as Rees and Weinstein (1983) have shown. In this way, the regional shift in manufacturing must be seen as the corollary of structural change in the United States economy. The manufacturing belt has gone into decline because its traditional resource-based industries have been eclipsed by the science-based industries of the post-industrial era.

Local trends in the distribution of employment

Accompanying these regional changes are some important shifts in the location of industry and employment at the local scale. In common with and both causing and reflecting movements of population, industry and employment are decentralizing from central cities to the suburbs and from the metropolitan to the non-metropolitan areas. Suburbanization is an established long-term pattern, but analysis of employment trends within the city suggests that the suburban component has grown especially rapidly over the last twenty years. In consequence, suburban employment in many cities now exceeds central city employment. For example, the suburban employment component in 1975 was approximately 60 per cent in Washington, San Francisco, and St Louis, and between 50 and 55 per cent in New York City, Philadelphia, and Baltimore (Muller, 1980). Generally, the move out was led by manufacturing and retail trade, but the specialized services of the metropolitan office industry remain tied to the central city. Levels of suburban economic development vary across the nation but the increasing size and diversity of their economic bases is now such that suburban areas must be regarded as "outer cities" in their own right. Non-metropolitan industrialization constitutes a new phase in the evolving economic geography of the nation (Lonsdale, 1979). The rate of increase in industrial employment in non-metropolitan areas has recently been well ahead of the metropolitan pace, and since about 1960 non-metropolitan areas have accounted for well over half of all new industrial jobs. The addition of nearly 2 million manufacturing jobs in rural and other smaller communities between 1962 and 1978 raised manufacturing employment from 3.9 to 5.7 million workers, an increase of almost 50 per cent. The share of the nation's manufacturing found in non-metropolitan areas increased from 24 to 29 per cent, not far behind their 31 per cent share of the nation's population.

The shift of employment and economic activity to the suburbs is explained by four main factors (Kirwan, 1981). First are changes in production processes in industry which necessitate large sites and single-storey manufacturing plants; second, abandonment of rail transport in favor of the new interstate and circumferential highways, and the consequent movement towards highway interchanges; third, the effect of outward population movement on the location of commercial activity; and fourth, the movement to the suburbs of the skilled labor force, coupled with the presence there of "captive", largely female, labor for light industrial and service activities. The fact that outward movement has been especially pronounced since the 1960s means that highway construction is probably the most important of these influences. The completion of the metropolitan freeway network greatly reduced the costs of intra-urban trucking, and although designed to bring city centers closer together, the system equally increased the accessibility of the suburbs. Rather than facilitating a revival of the inner areas, the freeways enabled more industry, and more population, to move out from the center.

This redistribution of industry and employment within the city underlines the increasing unattractiveness of central areas to manufacturing industry. For Berry and Cohen (1975) the central city has always possessed major disadvantages for goods producers, developing only because proximity meant lower transportation and communication costs for those independent specialists who had to interact frequently or intensively and could only do so on a face-to-face basis. But shortened distances also generated higher densities, costs of congestion, and higher rent, so that as soon as technology permitted, the metropolis was transformed to minimize these negative externalities. In a more extreme statement, Thompson (1975) suggests that the major industrial cities were not consciously built; they were formed from the agglomeration of manufacturing firms together with their labor pools. "We sort of woke up one day and there was Cleveland. There was Detroit, with four and a half million people, the biggest factory town on earth" (p. 189).

In contrast to suburbanization, the rise in industrial employment in non-metropolitan areas is a more recent and so less well understood phenomenon. Some growth in manufacturing is taking place adjacent to the edge of the city and so must be regarded as extreme suburbanization, but the extent of industrial development in areas remote from the metropolis is sufficient to justify claims that a "rural revival" is under way. For example, Kuehn's (1979) analysis of manufacturing change in the Ozarks showed that the same number (40 per cent) of new firms attracted to the area between 1967 and 1974 located in non-metropolitan areas which lacked cities as located in non-metropolitan areas on the fringe of the metropolis. For Seyler and Lonsdale (1979), a great many interdependent factors are responsible for non-metropolitan industrialization, including transportation and communications improvements, greater capital mobility, changes in industrial organization, the diffusion of urban values to the countryside, the real and perceived social and economic problems associated with large urban concentrations, and geographical differences in wage rates. A close correspondence necessarily exists between non-metropolitan population growth and non-metropolitan industrialization, although the nature of cause and effect is far from clear. For Kuehn (1979) changing space preferences among residents are of central importance. Increasing numbers of people are showing strong preferences for small towns and rural areas, trading off quality of environment against high earnings, and rural repopulation both provides labor and generates localized demand for industry and its products. As the locational conditions which created the compact and highly centralized city of the industrial era disappear, so the post-industrial economy is creating new distributions of industry and employment, involving suburban and non-metropolitan growth, at the local scale.

Conclusion

The most important point to emerge from this chapter is that recent changes in the location of industry and employment are the product of structural shifts in the United States economy. A new industrial structure has emerged since mid-century based upon electronics, aerospace, instruments, computers, drugs, optics, and plastics manufacture as leading sectors. Unlike the iron and steel, automobile engineering, and heavy metals industries of the industrial era, these growth industries have different raw material, capital and labor requirements and so are not constrained to the traditional coalfield, break-of-bulk, or market locations of the North-East and Lake Shore regions. Indeed, the obsolescent environments, high energy cost, and snowbelt climates of these areas are perceived as negative factors. Increased locational flexibility and improved national and local accessibility mean that these activities can locate more widely across the South and West and within the metropolis. A relative decline in the economic importance of the North-East is a long-term trend, but in recent years this has become absolute. Conversely, industry and employment in southern and western states and cities is expanding at an accelerating rate. In these ways, the post-industrial economy has added a new locational dimension to the industrial geography of the United States.

4

The post-industrial city

The social and economic trends identified in the preceding three
chapters are changing the geographical structure of the nation's
cities. Urban areas which were created through a centralization of
people and jobs are being transformed by powerful processes of
deconcentration. In place of a dense mass of people and firms
clustered tightly in rings around the Central Business District, out-
migration is spreading population, jobs, and services to the extremes of the metropolitan area and beyond. At the same time,
urban lifestyles, which were once determined by the size, density
and heterogeneity of the city population, increasingly reflect the
many combinations of class, ethnicity, and income that exist in
wider American society. These shifts and changes herald the
demise of a form of settlement which, with its associated social
geography, was a product of the industrial era. It is being succeeded by the post-industrial city.

As well as reducing the overall population size and economic
base of the metropolis, out-migration is creating marked geographical disparities within the city. Peaks of attraction and affluence
in the urban land use surface that once coincided with the nation's
Central Business Districts have become troughs of rejection and
decline, while the suburbs and exurbs have advanced in relative

prosperity. Underlying the complexities of population movements is a general outward shift of the wealthy and achievement-oriented, such that central cities are being abandoned to those in low status, low income, and minority racial groups. These distributional trends add a pronounced geographical dimension to the problems of service provision, poverty, and crime, that characterize American society. They are fundamental causes of the crisis in the city that is an established and increasing feature of contemporary urban America.

A range of policies has been developed over the past twenty years to try to resolve the growing problems of the nation's urban areas. Public intervention in the city was traditionally restricted to civic improvement and housing schemes, but this has been overtaken by a succession of urban aid programs designed to rehabilitate the social and physical fabric of the metropolis. Assistance is made available both directly to individuals, via fiscal and welfare schemes, and indirectly by providing financial help to local businesses and government. The geopolitical fragmentation of local administration, which has resulted in many urban services being seriously under-funded, however, contributes to the difficulty. The severity of the urban crisis and the wide range of responses means that cities have largely replaced depressed regions as the nation's major problem areas.

A different role for cities is an expected corollary of the passage into post-industrialism. Cities exist to serve the needs of society, and as structural changes occur in society, so corresponding shifts take place in the organization and functions of metropolitan areas. Although general throughout the nation, these shifts are inevitably most pronounced, and so generate the greatest frictions, among those northern cities that are grounded most firmly in the preceding industrial era. This chapter is concerned with the existing and the emerging urban pattern. Specifically, it analyzes the emerging spatial organization, and some of the problems of the post-industrial American city.

The commercial structure of the city

Most large American cities have a clearly discernible and highly similar spatial form. Physical geography characteristically imposes certain constraints by way of relief features, rivers, coasts, and shorelines, although the underlying gridiron pattern owes most to nineteenth-century surveys and planning. Against this backcloth, a cluster of skyscrapers and other high buildings housing offices and hotels delimits the Central Business District, widths of roads and the alignment of canals and railroads demarcate the major arterial routes, while concentrations of factories, shops, and housing identify the industrial, retailing, and residential areas (Figure 4.1). Alongside selected streets are the elongated strip developments of drive-ins, gas stations, and motels that are so distinctive a feature of the American city, while around the central area is a fragmented fringe containing blighted residences, wholesaling districts, and industrial sectors. This in turn is encircled by an inner city zone of old properties occupied predominantly by low income earners, racial and ethnic minorities. The morphological uniformity of the suburban rings is periodically interrupted by large enclosed shopping malls and low-rise office-service complexes each with their extensive parking lots. Low density of development is the overriding feature contributing to the vast areal extent of the city, and the dividing line between urban and rural is vague and imprecise. External links are maintained by the interstate highways and their connecting urban expressways which thread their way through the outer city and from the busy peripherally sited airport.

Many of the structural elements in the highly idealized model are exhibited in the geography of Oklahoma City (population 1980, 403,000) as described by Knox (1982). As a twentieth century creation, Oklahoma City is predominantly a product of the automobile age, a feature which is reflected in its overall layout. Beyond the relatively compact inner city, the morphology is characteristically low density, dominated by detached single-storey dwellings. Extending some 45 kilometers east-west, and 30 kilometers north-south, the urban area is interlaced by a network of four-and six-lane radial and circumferential highways and is organized around a number of nodal sub-centers including Bethany, Moore, Midwest City, and Del City (Figure 4.2). As in many other American cities, retailing facilities are decentralized, concentrated upon arterial highways, in shopping plazas adjacent to highway access points, and in air-conditioned malls such as Crossroads Mall, at the intersection of Interstate Highways 240 and 35. Similarly, most of the metropolitan area's employment is located at suburban sites leaving the Central

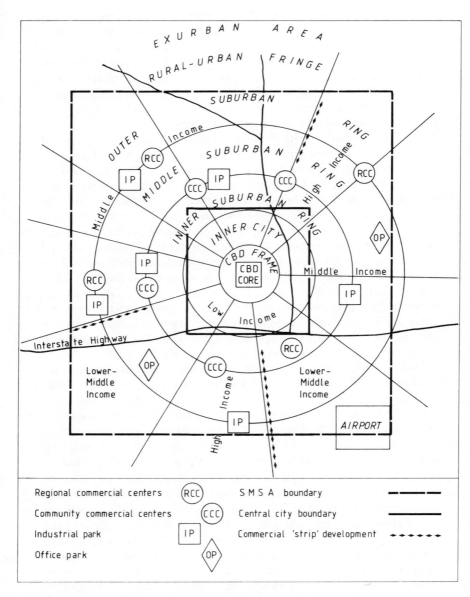

Figure 4.1   *The spatial structure of the post-industrial city*

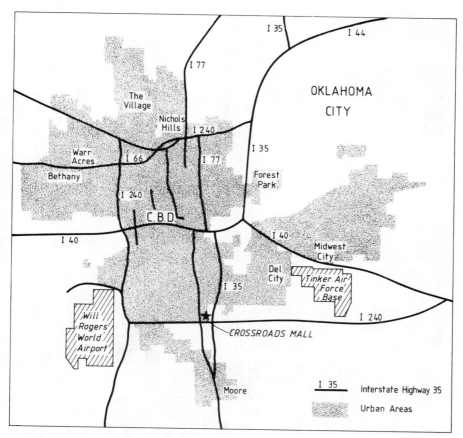

Figure 4.2   *Oklahoma City*

Business District as an island of office blocks, expensive hotels, and a conference center. These are surrounded by a no-man's land of warehouses, stockyards, and vacant and half-demolished buildings once occupied by businesses and cheap housing.

Beyond the Central Business District and its surrounding zone-in-transition are decaying neighborhoods occupied by Indians and poor Whites. About 3 kilometers from the center, these neigbor-hoods give way to areas of newer, sounder housing, although the transition is interrupted on the northern edge of the inner city by a narrow zone of institutional uses including several hospitals and

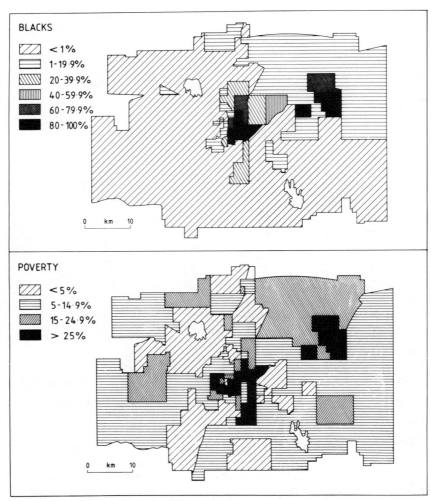

Figure 4.3   *Oklahoma City: social characteristics*
Source: *Knox (1982, p. 74).*

the state administrative complex. Beyond this inner core there is a high degree of residential segregation. The city's Black population is located almost exclusively in a narrow sector extending from the center, while the elderly are concentrated in inner city neighborhoods (Figure 4.3). The city's poor are similarly clustered around

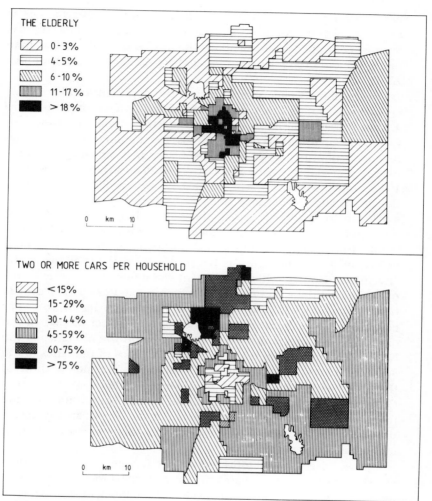

Figure 4.3　Continued

the center, although there is a concentration in the north-eastern quarter. The highest status and the most affluent groups are localized in a sector extending north-west from the Central Business District with a heartland in the exclusive municipality of Nicolls Hills. For Knox (1982) these residential patterns are reflected in the geography of car ownership. More than three quarters of the households in the Nicolls Hills area have two or more cars, whereas in most central city neigborhoods this proportion falls to less than one-third and in the deprived inner city neighborhoods it is almost zero.

The combined effects of historical development and economic specialization mean that though the elements identified in Figure 4.1 are present in almost all American cities, there are important variations of urban structure across the nation. New York City reached a population of 350,000 just before 1840, Philadelphia some twenty years later, Washington DC in 1920, and Dallas in the early 1940s, and these differences of lifestage are inevitably reflected in the urban fabric. The most obvious contrasts involve the housing stock which is oldest among the cities of the nation's historic metropolitan core, and in the nineteenth-century industrial centers (Table 4.1). Nearly two-thirds of the housing in Boston was built before 1940, but the figure is below one-quarter for all six of the "twentieth century" cities. Important variations also exist in terms of single unit detached dwellings which range from 31 per cent of the housing stock in New York and northern New Jersey, to 73 per cent in Seattle. Central city densities further reflect the age of the city, the heavy concentration of population in the old cities of the North-East contrasting with the lower densities of the cities of the South and West. These indices of differences are merely three of the many which are mapped by Abler and Adams (1976) in their *Comparative Atlas of America's Great Cities*. They underline the need to qualify general statements about the American city according to the age, economic and social characteristics of each individual place.

At the heart of the representative city, the Central Business District dominates the urban landscape. Its most important characteristic is the exceptionally high value of the block of land which it occupies, which in turn accounts for both its limited spatial extent and its vertical development. High land values arise out of competition between those in commerce, retailing, and the hotel business for location at the point of maximum vehicle and pedestrian access in the city. It is from the most central location that enterprises commanding the widest markets and with highest sales are likely to generate greatest profits. The premium which is placed upon centrality leads to a highly compact Central Business District in

Table 4.1 *Housing and population density characteristics of America's great cities*

	SMSA housing		Central city(ies) population density (per sq. km)
	% built before 1940	% single unit detached	
The nation's metropolitan core			
Boston	64	42	5400
New York–Northern New Jersey	53	31	10,175
Philadelphia	50	37	5900
Hartford: Connecticut Valley	40	72	3500
Nineteenth-century ports			
Baltimore	40	40	4500
New Orleans	34	52	1200
San Francisco–Oakland	37	52	6100[1]
			2600[2]
Nineteenth-century inland centers and ports			
Pittsburgh	54	66	3600
St Louis	42	61	3940
Cleveland	46	57	3800
Chicago	48	45	5800
Detroit	37	69	4200
Minneapolis–St Paul	39	63	2700
Seattle	30	73	2500
Twentieth-century cities			
Dallas–Fort Worth	18	71	1200[3]
			730[4]
Houston	15	72	610
Los Angeles	25	62	2350
Miami–Miami Beach	15	56	3800[5]
			5250[6]
Atlanta	18	66	1470
Washington DC	22	43	4750

Note: [1] San Francisco [2] Oakland [3] Dallas [4] Fort Worth [5] Miami [6] Miami Beach.
Source: Abler and Adams (1976).

which the tallness of the buildings reflects, in part, the high cost of sites, but also the prestige derived from owning and occuping the highest skyscraper in the city.

Within the downtown areas there are pronounced variations in the intensity of land use and the types of activities which are carried on. These reflect differences in the importance of centrality to firms, and their abilities to compete for space and location. A basic distinction may be drawn between "core" activities consisting of high-class offices, shops, and hotels which are concentrated around the peak land value intersection, and the surrounding "frame" area of more mixed land uses (Horwood and Boyce, 1959). The characteristics of these two areas differentiate the Central Business District internally in terms of function, building height, mode of movement, and morphology.

The core of the Central Business District is the area of most expensive land and, correspondingly, of the greatest intensity of land use in the city. It is dominated by prestige offices and commercial activities, and supporting hotels, shops, and restaurants. Lying at the very center of the city, it is the focus of convergence for mass transit systems and as a consequence has a high daytime but a negligible nighttime population. Walking distances are critical in restricting the spread of the core, and great reliance is placed upon the elevator for internal movement. The core has the highest retail sales density per unit of ground area in the city. Moreover, with its concentration of corporate decision-making functions it is the commercial center for the urban and regional business community.

The frame is an area of mixed land uses surrounding the inner core. Its typical activities include business services, wholesaling, warehousing, light manufacturing, and various kinds of transport facilities such as trucking and intercity transportation terminals. Intermingled with these are low quality residences, especially old multi-family houses, tenements, and transient rooming houses. This mixture gives rise to a less intensive use of land than in the core. The vertical expression is not nearly as exaggerated, but the horizontal scale is more extended and is geared to movement, parking, and the handling of goods. The land use pattern in the frame in fact reflects the overriding importance of the motor vehicle which enables many activities to occupy low rent sites in close proximity to the core. Despite the outward orientation towards the rest of the city and beyond, most of the uses in the frame have close linkages with activities in the core. This is especially true of warehousing, distribution, and a wide range of business services such as printing and transport. These connections mean that although comprising two distinct morphological areas, the Central Business District is an integrated functional region.

Despite a decline relative to its heyday in the industrial era, the Central Business District remains the largest single concentration of commercial activity in most cities. The main reason is that loss of retail trade has been offset since the mid-1960s by a major growth in office buildings and jobs, a boom which is evidenced by the construction of modern glass-fronted high-rise buildings alongside the early twentieth-century skyscrapers in the downtown area. Many Central Business Districts increased their office space by over 75 per cent between 1960 and 1972, while in some, including San Francisco and Minneapolis–St Paul, the increase was over 100 per cent (Manners, 1974). In the New York metropolitan area, 111 million square feet of office floor space was constructed between 1960 and 1975 and another 2.6 million square feet was under construction in 1975. Manhattan alone had 227 million square feet in 1975 which was an increase of 84 per cent over 1960. The massive financial investments implied by these totals were made in the downtown area as entrepreneurs attempted to bolster its traditional economic strengths and to capitalize on the locational advantages of the Central Business District for office functions. They were paralleled by expenditure by city governments across the nation who attempted to stem the decline of the Central Business District by building conference and convention centers, hotel complexes, and enclosed shopping malls in their downtown areas.

The Central Business District occupies the dominant position in a hierarchy of commercial areas in the city as Berry (1966) has shown (Figure 4.4). Each tier differs in terms of the variety of goods and services provided, and the size of markets served by its constituent centers. Outside the Central Business District, the highest level is that of regional centers which offer the full depth and variety of convenience and comparison goods together with some more specialized lines. They lack only the highly exclusive shopping which is to be found in the central area. Regional commercial centers normally have at least one major department

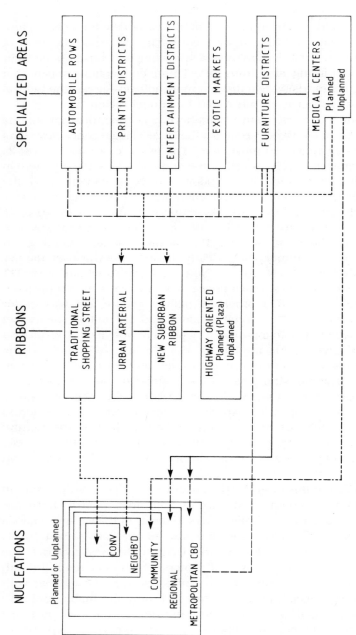

Figure 4.4   *Commercial hierarchies in the city*
Source: *Berry (1963, p. 6)*

store as location leader, and range from 27,500 to 93,000 square meters in area. They provide up to 8000 car parking spaces, and serve a minimum population of 150,000 (Kivell, 1972). Community centers have the full complement of convenience goods but a more limited range of shopping goods, being restricted in this category to the merchandise sold by variety and clothing stores, and small furniture and domestic appliance outlets. Typically, they offer 9300 to 27,500 square meters of selling space and cater for 50-100,000 people. The day-to-day convenience goods requirements of up to 50,000 are provided by neighborhood centers. Grocery stores, small supermarkets, laundries, dry cleaners, barbers and beauty shops, and small restaurants are the types most usually represented. At the lowest level in the hierarchy are the street corner convenience centers. The most ubiquitous element in the urban commercial system, they have merely three or four low threshold businesses, the grocery and drugstore being the most common. The growth of this hierarchy of planned shopping centers is very much a feature of the last quarter century. It reflects the adjustment of the retail sector to the changing distribution of population in the city, and to the transport changes associated with the development of expressway systems. Chicago alone had sixty-two planned shopping centers by 1962 and by the mid-1970s, fifteen of these, all in the suburbs, were classified as regional centers (Berry, 1976a).

The work of Berry (1963) suggested that a variety of ribbon and specialized area developments completed the commercial profile of Chicago and were probably present in most large American cities. Ribbon developments are the most conspicuous element in urban structure since they form the backdrop to the most well-traveled routes through the urban area. Most cities have a number of traditional shopping streets developed in the pre-automobile era along which are to be found a range of varied and long-established retail and commercial outlets. Surrounded by streets of older properties, their continuing viability is heavily dependent upon the convenience goods services they provide to a captive local market. More recent ribbon developments reflect the post-war growth in car ownership which gave rise to highway-oriented developments serving the transient demands of the passing motorist and truck driver. Functions located along highways and arterial routes include gas stations and service stations, drive-ins, ice cream parlors, and motels. Most of these outlets are owned, or operated under a franchise system, by national corporations so that strip developments across America consist of the same mix of familar trade names. Best Western, Holiday Inn, Ramada Inn, Travel Lodge, and Motel 6 are among the most ubiquitous in the motel sector, while MacDonald's, Burger King, Wendy's, Dairy Queen, Pizza Hut, and Kentucky Fried Chicken are the most common fast food outlets to be found along the strip. For the most part, ribbons are uncontrolled developments, although along some of the new intra-urban highways service plazas of a planned nature have been constructed.

Specialized retail areas in the city are formed by recognizable clusters of establishments of the same business type or of function-ally interrelated business types within the area. They are usually freestanding in location although they may take the form of alike and adjacent uses within a large commercial center. Specialized areas are of many diverse kinds with the most common being the automobile row consisting of a cluster of new and used car and truck dealers, and facilities for parts, repairs, and servicing, strung out along streets in the city. Other types present in Chicago and probably present in other large cities include medical, printing, household furnishing, and entertainment districts, and the exotic markets which service the need for particular ethnic and racial groups. These areas are held together by close linkages among their constituent establishments from which are derived economies of operation. Their geographical concentration also assists trade by facilitating comparative shopping.

The social and residential mosaic

A high level of differentiation is the overriding characteristic of the social geography of the post-industrial city. Far from being a uniform entity, sets of zones, communities or neighborhoods are normally distinguishable in terms of physical appearance or mor-phology, population composition, and lifestyle. Together these comprise a residential and social mosaic that is repeated from city to city across the nation. In part, this is a product of urban growth which added a succession of peripheral rings of development to the city, so that building age declines steeply with distance away from the center (Figure 4.5). It also has more general structural origins. As a microcosm of a wider world, the social geography of the contemporary city reflects the divisions and differences in post-industrial American society.

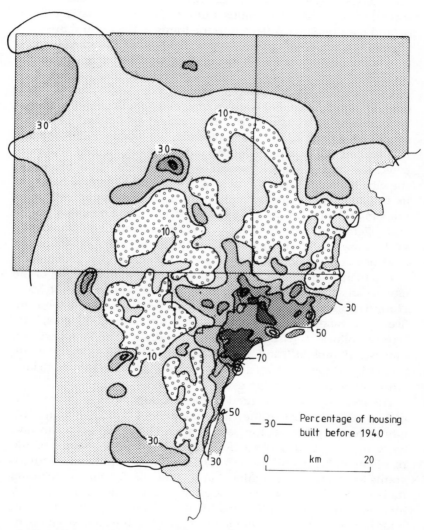

Figure 4.5 *Detroit: age of buildings*

Although it is some sixty years since Burgess (1925) first drew attention to the ring structure of the industrial city, elements of a concentric zonal pattern are still recognizable in many urban areas today. Over half a century of growth and change has shifted the boundaries between some of Burgess's regions and has blurred several of his social distinctions, but the underlying spatial pattern of land uses remains. Adjacent to the frame of the Central Business District is a region of old properties that formed the suburb at the turn of the century. Once an area of some wealth, it is now a zone of residential dereliction in which much of the original housing stock has been subdivided, converted or cleared to make way for business, light industrial and warehousing uses, and for road construction. Indeed dilapidation and decay mean that slum conditions prevail over parts of the area. Although the waves of immigration that fuelled the expansion of the industrial city have now diminished, the area is still the major reception zone for those moving to the city. It also provides, because of the age and obsolete nature of its buildings, poor quality and cheap accommodation for householders and industry. As a consequence, low income groups, ethnic and religious minorities, or marginal firms are strongly represented in the area. The zone in transition is essentially an area of mixed land use containing a variety of social and economic activities.

The highly varied character of the central and inner areas of the city means that they house people from a wide range of backgrounds and with very different lifestyles. For Gans (1962a) there are five basic types of inner city resident: the "urban villagers," the "cosmopolites," the "unmarrieds or childless," the "trapped and downward mobile," and the "deprived." Despite living in close proximity in the same area of the city they differ in terms of class, ethnicity, and stage in life cycle.

The most well documented of these groups are the urban villagers, so called because they are members of small, intimate, and ethnic communities in the central area. Their characteristics and ways of life are described by Gans (1962b) in his study of the residents of West End, Boston. The area was populated by immigrants from a variety of national and ethnic backgrounds including Italians, Poles, Irish, Greeks, Ukranians, Albanians, and Jews; low incomes, an absence of occupational skills and qualifications, and poor housing were common features. Behind the somewhat offensive facade of the area, which was strongly influenced by the dilapidated state of the buildings, the vacant lots, and the garbage on the streets, Gans found a friendly, intimate and close-knit community, reminiscent of that which exists in small towns and rural areas. The family and religion were important elements in social organization, and the sharing of common values was also encouraged by residential stability and the diverse network of personal acquaintances. Everyone might not know everyone else, but as they did know something about everyone the net effect was the same, especially within each ethnic group. Between groups, common residence, sharing of facilities, and the constant struggle against absentee landlords, created enough solidarity to maintain a friendly spirit. Although for many families problems of unemployment, finance, illness, education, and bereavement were never far away, neighbors and friends were always on hand to provide assistance and support. The wider relevance of Gans' observations may be criticized on the grounds that the West End was populated by predominantly first generation immigrants who had yet to be exposed to the full impact of urban living, but similar findings have been reported elsewhere. Studies of lifestyles in Chicago and New York (Gans, 1962b) suggest that urban village communities analogous to those in Boston probably exist in the central area of most large America cities.

Gans' second group, the "cosmopolites" includes students, artists, writers, musicians, and entertainers, as well as intellectuals and professionals who live in the inner city in order to be near the special cultural facilities of the center. Many are unmarried or childless, but others rear children in the city especially if they have the income to support servants or governesses. Still others, though having an out-of-town residence, maintain a cosmopolitan lifestyle from a pied-à-terre in the inner city. The "unmarrieds or childless" are divided into two subtypes depending upon the permanence or transience of their status. The temporarily unmarried or childless live in the inner city for only a limited time and, upon marriage or starting a family, they leave for the suburbs, whereas the permanently unmarried live in the inner city for the remainder of their lives, their housing depending upon income. The former typically includes students or young people who share a downtown flat or apartment away from parents but close to jobs or entertainment opportunities. The fourth group are the "trapped and downward mobiles" who are people who stay behind when a neighborhood is invaded by non-residential land uses or by lower status immigrants, because they cannot afford to move or are otherwise bound to their present location. Those who started life in a high-class position, but who have been forced down in the socio-economic hierarchy and in the quality of their accommodation because of personal circumstances, are typical members of this group. It also includes old people, living out their existence on small pensions. The final group is the "deprived" population: the very poor, the emotionally disturbed or otherwise handicapped, broken families and the non-White population. They occupy the most dilapidated housing and most blighted neighborhoods to which they are restricted by the market, although among them are some for whom the slum is a refuge or temporary stop-over while they save money for a house in the outer city.

The form of the residential areas which extend beyond the zone in transition owes much to the influence of transportation. Today's midtown areas are essentially the early century streetcar suburbs, created by the combined efforts of the developers/speculators and the trolley bus companies. They consist of gridded streets of uniformly styled, predominantly detached medium density housing. In spatial terms they are comparatively restricted although later linear extensions, created by the inter-war transit systems, are evident in a number of cities. The contemporary suburbs date from the immediate post-war period when large-scale development at what was then the edge of the city took place. They are largely a product of the massive decentralization of the urban population that was made possible by extensions of suburban rail networks and increases in private car ownership. Suburban growth was especially fast in the decade following 1945 when post-war prosperity, combined with a rapid increase in the rate of household formation, generated enormous demands for housing. In common with the streetcar period, the most important feature of residential construction was that comparatively few designs were employed so the morphological uniformity of the suburbs was maintained. The geographical extent of the largest American cities is now such that the influence of the Central Business District is minimal. As a consequence there is as much variation of population composition and lifestyle within the suburbs as there is between the suburbs and the center.

In analyzing the contemporary city, Muller (1981, p. 70), following

Table 4.2 *Selected socio-economic characteristics of representative suburban lifestyle community types, 1970*

| Variable | Exclusive upper income | Middle-income family | | Working class | Cosmopolitan suburb |
	Grosse Pointe Shores, Mich.	Upper Darien Conn.	Lower Levittown, NY	Milpitas, Calif.	Princeton, NJ
Median family income	$32,565	$22,172	$13,083	$11,543	$12,182
Per cent families > $25,000	60.4	41.9	5.7	1.7	18.0
Per cent families < $15,000	19.1	29.6	64.0	75.8	59.8
Per cent families in poverty	2.1	2.4	3.0	5.3	5.2
Per cent Black	0.2	0.5	0.1	5.2	10.0
Median age	41.3	32.1	24.0	20.9	28.4
Per cent population < 18	30.3	35.5	41.4	46.4	16.3
Per cent population > 65	12.4	7.8	3.6	2.1	10.6
Per cent same address 1965	59.5	60.3	75.1	31.5	34.2
Per cent population 3–34 in school	80.3	71.0	63.0	55.3	67.4
Per cent high school graduates	83.1	83.1	64.2	63.6	76.5
Per cent women in labor force	20.8	34.5	41.9	45.5	49.4
Per cent professional and technical workers	28.3	25.7	13.6	16.9	37.6
Per cent managerial/administrative workers	31.6	25.2	9.4	5.2	7.5
Per cent operatives	0.8	4.3	7.6	18.5	2.8

Source: Muller (1981 p. 79).

Suttles (1975, p. 265–71) and Berry (1973, p. 65), identified four basic community forms within the suburbs: the exclusive affluent apartment complex; middle-class family areas; low income, ethnic centered working-class communities; and cosmopolitan centers. The socio-economic characteristics of these types in terms of income, population stability, age structure, and education are illustrated by data for representative communities in Grosse Pointe Shores (Michigan), Darien (Connecticut), Levittown (New York), Milpitas (California), and Princeton (New Jersey) (Table 4.2).

The high income suburbs are characteristically located in areas possessing both physical isolation and the choicest environmental amenities, around water, trees, and higher ground. Since houses are built on large plots and are well fenced, neighboring is difficult, and people keep in touch by participation in local social networks. The latter are tightly structured around organizations such as churches, country and golf clubs, and newcomers to the community are carefully screened for their social credentials before being accepted. Exclusiveness is reinforced by private schools and by the emphasis placed upon class traditions. A recent development in high income areas is the growth of luxury apartment and condominium complexes which attract increasing numbers of affluent singles, families, and senior citizens.

Middle-class family suburbs are located as close as possible to the high status residential enclaves of the most affluent. They are populated by middle-income groups which are arranged into nuclear family units. The management of children is a central concern and most local social contact occurs though family-oriented formal organizations such as school associations, children's societies, and sports clubs. Despite the closer spacing of homes and these integrating activities, middle-class suburbanites are not communally cohesive to any great degree. Emphasis upon family privacy, and freedom to aggressively pursue upward social mobility, does not encourage the development of extensive local social ties. Neighboring (mostly child related) is limited and selective, and even socializing with relatives is infrequent. Most social interaction revolves around a non-local network of selected friends, widely distributed in suburban space. The insular single family house and dependence on the automobile for all trips accommodate these preferences and foster a congruence between lifestyle and the spatial arrangement of the residential environment.

Outside the central city, the working class and poor areas are predominantly found in the innermost pre-automobile suburbs, and adjacent to industrial areas and railroads. For Muller (p. 71), working-class suburban lifestyles differ from middle-class suburban lifestyles in a number of ways. Whereas middle-class suburbs stress the nuclear family unit, socialization with friends, and a minimum of local contact, working-class neighborhoods accentuate the extended family, frequent home entertaining of relatives rather than acquaintances, and a great deal of informal local social interaction outside the home. The latter is reflected by the importance of local meeting places such as churches, taverns, and street corners. Rather than a breakdown of social contact, these informal networks introduce an important element of social cohesion into working-class suburbs. Moreover, local area attachment is reinforced by a person-oriented rather than a material- or achievement-oriented outlook. Working-class suburbanites have no great hopes of getting ahead with their largely blue-collar jobs, have few aspirations as regards upward social mobility, and therefore view their present home and community as a place of permanent settlement.

Muller's fourth category of suburban lifestyle is the suburban cosmopolitan center. It is distinguished by communities of professionals, intellectuals, students, artists, and writers who participate in far-flung intra-and inter-metropolitan social networks and communities of interest. As theaters, music and arts facilities, fine restaurants, and other cultural activities have deconcentrated, so cosmopolitan centers have spread throughout the city, and lifestyles that were once the preserve of inner areas have become predominantly suburban. This expansion has been assisted by the opening of branch campuses of universities and colleges which provide a cultural and intellectual focus in the suburbs.

The very different types of community and associated lifestyles that can be identified in the contemporary American suburbs suggest that location is unimportant as a controlling factor. What differentiates suburban communities is occupation, social class and ethnicity, which define a set of constraints within which people choose which lifestyle to follow. Especially important are considerations of income which determine both residential location and patterns of social interaction. The suburbs, like the central city, offer a range of distinctive niches within a mosaic culture which is increasingly dominating urban America. Lifestyles are not determined by place of residence in the city, rather they reflect the socio-economic characteristics of the population.

The mosaic of social milieux in the city reflects the many combinations of socio-personal characteristics that are possible in the modern world. Social diversity exists because all of the major dimensions along which American society is differentiated have actually widened since the industrial era. Despite the overall reduction in numbers admitted, the immigration of Phillipinos, Mexicans, Koreans, Puerto Ricans, West Indians, and Vietnamese in the post-war period has added considerably to the racial and ethnic mix of the population. It has also increased the variety of main-stream religions and cultures. The range of lifestyles has been further extended by the proliferation of "dropout," "activist," "secular," and "back to the land" movements, as recognized and described by Watson (1979). The popularity of alternative religions is a related development. More general changes in social attitudes since the 1960s have led to the tolerance, if not acceptance, of lesbianism and homosexuality, while the rising divorce rate has added a new category of marital status to the social statistics. The expansion of universities and colleges has created an educated elite, but has widened the gap which separates those with degrees from those with little formal schooling. A similar increase in differentials distinguishes the skilled and unskilled, the affluent and impoverished. Finally, the general increase in longevity has given additional importance to age as a diagnostic variable. As yet, the melting-pot effect has been unable to produce homogeneity: rather, post-industrial America is an increasingly complex plural society.

Such social diversity gives rise to complex sets of attractions and aversions which find expression in neighborhood formation. The mechanisms involved are explained in relation to the locational decisions taken by households and firms. For Cox (1973), each decision-making unit has a set of resources such as personnel, capital, and land which it allocates to its activities so as to maximize utility. Thus, in fulfilling the needs of its members, a household commits, within a fixed budget, sums and resources to shelter, home improvements, food, transport, and so on. An important characteristic of this allocation process is, however, that individuals' utilities are not independent: what is in the interests of some may benefit but may also be to the detriment of others. For example, decorating the home will be to the advantage of the individual householder and to the neighborhood, but whereas the purchase of a car may benefit one household in terms of improved mobility, it generates pollution and obstruction to the inconvenience and annoyance of another. Two types of externality effect are recognized. The first is "public behavior externalities" which cover levels of property maintenance, crime, public comportment, and the activities of one's children; the second is "status externalities" which are those generated by the social and ethnic standing of households. For Cox, such side-effects establish a set of likes and dislikes in the city. It is in response to these qualities that urban spatial structure is explained.

Although there is no evidence that social groups view externalities in markedly different ways, the wide variations of income, culture, racial, ethnic, educational, and occupational characteristics of the United States population mean that levels of achievement of externalities vary considerably. Cox interprets the emergence of areal divisions within the city as a response to demands for accessibility to those who successfully provide positive externalities, and a demand for physical distance from those perceived to provide negative externalities. Thus location is sought close to groups who maintain the value of their properties, are socially responsible, and who expect and require similar patterns of behavior in their children, whereas deviant, criminal, and low status households are avoided. For Berry (1973), the individual searching for identity in a mass society seeks to minimize disorder by living in a neighborhood in which life is comprehensible and social relations predictable.

> He seeks an enclave of relative homogeneity: a predictable lifestyle; a territory free from status competition because his neighbors are "just like him;" a turf compatible in outlook because his neighbors are at similar stages in the life cycle; a safe area, free from status challenging ethnic or racial minorities". (p. 51)

The net result is a residential segregation of the city which reflects the social and economic divisions within American society.

Neighborhood formation and change is helped by that distinctively American social dynamic, the overriding commitment to social advancement. McClelland (1961) has pointed out that the drive for achievement is a variable of key importance within mainstream American culture, a culture in which status and self respect come from what a person does, in the material world, rather than from his ancestry or his holiness. It explains the importance of children "getting ahead" and "improving themselves" through education, and of workers ascending the job hierarchy. Earnings must be spent on the best possible homes and material possessions, in the best possible neighborhoods. Any increase in job or financial status must be matched by a move to a better neighborhood in which the new and high status lifestyle may be pursued. This process of mobility is lubricated by the construction industry which tends to build large-scale residential developments which are homogeneous in style, price, and quality. These filter in those from a common background and exclude those who are different. A further factor is the finance and real estate industry which tends to reinforce neighborhood character by operating a discriminatory system of housing allocation as Palm (1976) has shown.

The contemporary urban crisis

Underlying the detailed differences of population and lifestyle between urban neighborhoods on the local scale are more pronounced contrasts of social and economic condition between the inner and outer city. Central area–suburban differentials were a feature of the industrial metropolis, but the greater level of overall urban prosperity, the pre-eminence of the Central Business District and the beneficial effects of immigration into the inner area, meant that the gradient was neither steep nor especially serious. Indeed the central city was the major zone of affluence in the metropolis and in the nation. The decentralization of population and industry has, however, inverted this pattern. As cities are turning themselves inside out, so the area of greatest wealth has shifted to the suburbs and beyond, with far-reaching implications for the viability of the central area, and indeed, in some cases, of the city as a whole.

The most important consequence of decentralization is that areas of out-migration have become zones of concentrated deprivation and decay. As affluent groups moved out of the inner rings in increasing numbers during the 1960s and 1970s, so vast tracts of the central city were pitched into a cycle of accelerated decline. Once elegant single family homes in high-status neighborhoods became, in rapid succession, residences of middle-class families, apartments for the lower middle class, rooming houses for the poor, and were finally abandoned. The vacuum left by out-movement was filled by Blacks and other minority racial and ethnic groups, keen to escape from the ancient slums, who moved as tenants into the former all-White areas. The only cost which owners could reduce to adjust to the fall in rental income was maintenance, so levels of upkeep and repair were minimal or non-existent, leading to further deterioration. Low level uses in turn led to a loss of confidence on the part of insurance companies and lenders who feared that the value of housing was falling faster than the value of mortgages. First on a selective basis, particular houses, certain blocks on certain streets, and then, area-wide by blanket "red-lining," insurance was refused and conventional financing withdrawn so that a normal real estate market ceased to exist for the affected areas. As a consequence, speculators moved in, acquiring houses at greatly deflated prices for resale to the poor. Although the progressive takeover of central cities by low income groups, racial and ethnic minorities, the elderly, the unemployed, and single-parent families, is a general phenomenon observable in most large American cities, it is most pronounced, and has most serious implications, in the declining cities of the North-East. A combination of general economic decline and an antiquated housing stock means that the processes of White flight, accelerated housing devaluation, and minority replacement, are most powerful in the industrial metropolises of the frostbelt. Many Southern and Western cities, in contrast, are prosperous and are expanding and have a range of modern housing which remains attractive. In some regions the "urban crisis" is restricted to comparatively small pockets of deprivation and decay in the city. Elsewhere it affects the city as a whole.

The disparities of social, economic and environmental conditions in the city are not helped by the geography of public service provision. Far from being a single geopolitical entity with one set of problems and a single means of resolving them, the American city is fragmented into a large number of jurisdictions. Generalization about structure is difficult because patterns vary widely, but a distinction between counties, townships, municipalities, and special districts exists in most states (Johnston, 1982). Each area covers a different size of territory and has a different set of responsibilities, some of which are accepted by delegation from higher levels in the local government hierarchy.

The most basic unit is the county, a form of local government present in all but one state (Rhode Island). In rural areas, counties are very much administrative arms of the state, providing law enforcement, judicial administration, maintenance of roads, supervision of public health, and administration of public welfare and agricultural extension programs. Where population densities are larger and the county contains nucleated settlements of some size, further services such as libraries and health facilities are commonly provided. In counties covering urban areas, further facilities still might be required, such as an airport, cultural and recreational services, land use control, street paving, cleaning and lighting, piped water, and waste disposal. All these services may be provided by the county government either directly, or by buying from other local governments or from private companies. In twenty-one predominantly north-eastern states, counties are subdivided into townships. Their functions are few and relatively insignificant although they vary markedly from state to state. For example, in Michigan, township governments provide cemeteries and volunteer fire departments, water supplies and street lighting, whereas in Illinois they are responsible only for road maintenance, property assessment, and the support of indigents (Johnston, 1982).

Within the counties are the municipalities, densely populated areas that have been legally incorporated under a variety of names such as cities, towns or villages, to provide local government services independent of those of the encompassing county. Incorporation is by the state government in response to a public petition and poll of its affected voters, and the functions of the municipal government are specified in its charter. More local still are the special districts, most of which are *ad hoc* bodies created for a specific function. The most common form of special district is the school district which in twenty-three states has complete autonomy over education within its territory (Johnston, 1982). Other special districts cover a wide range of functions of which fire protection, drainage, and the provision and maintenance of parks, are the most common. In 1977 there were 79,862 local government units in the United States, one for every 2800 of the population. There were also 490,265 elected local government officials, an average of 6.1 per unit, or one elected office for every 441 persons.

The problems of the city are exacerbated by this fragmentation because many jurisdictions are seriously under-resourced. Generally, the capacity of local government to provide public sector services depends upon the tax resources available within its boundaries, but since demand for services is often inversely related to the ability to pay, needs commonly go unmet in the areas covered by one authority, while elsewhere, tax resources are far from fully exploited. This situation characterizes the relationship of central cities and suburbs in the United States, and has been described by Cox (1973) as the "central city–suburban fiscal disparities problem." It refers to the imbalance between needs for government-provided public services and the tax resources with which to fund them.

Problems of provision arise because central areas generate high levels of demand for public services, but have only a low yield tax base. This situation is largely a result of the concentration in the central city of low income groups, ethnic minorities, crime, an aging population, and fire-prone housing, and is increased by migration and commuting trends. Central areas have a tendency to lose high value, high tax-paying businesses and activities, and to replace them by low income, low yield uses. Similarly, more daily movements take place by suburban residents to the center than of central residents to the suburbs, and this imposes a further burden of demands on the central city in the form of parking and transport terminal costs.

Fiscal collapse in decaying central areas is a general characteristic of United States cities as Alcaly and Memelstein (1977), Tabb (1977), and Hill (1977) have shown. It is especially pronounced in the older larger metropolises where the central area has to carry the additional burden of supporting nationally prestigious services such as libraries, zoos, centers for the performing arts, and many of the social costs associated with the headquarters offices of major corporations. The ways in which services are funded and municipal boundaries are drawn means that, in some areas, fiscal collapse, far from being a central area problem, is a city-wide phenomenon. The situation was in fact reached in New York City in 1975 when the city was declared bankrupt.

The roots of New York City's fiscal problems are representative of the same factors affecting other large central cities of the North-East and North Central regions. In recent years, these cities have absorbed new rural in-migrants from the South and South-West and from Puerto Rico. In the East, the stream has been heavily

Southern Black and Puerto Rican while in the North Central cities it has been primarily Southern Black and Mexican American. Also, as a result of modern transportation, middle-class families with school-age children have increasingly moved to the suburbs leaving the aged, who are less able to cope with dependency upon the automobile and with home maintenance, in the central city.

These migrational trends made New York City a center for groups dependent on public services. Between 1950 and 1970, the proportion of the city's population over the age of 65 increased from 8 per cent to 12 per cent, while the proportion of the city's families with incomes below the national median income level rose from 36 per cent to 49 per cent. Although population remained almost static over the period, the industrial base declined significantly: private sector jobs fell from 3.1 million in 1960 to 2.8 million in 1975. A further factor affecting the city's fiscal circumstances was the onset of national recession which by depressing the level of retail trade, restricted the sales tax yield. At the same time, high unemployment increased the number of families eligible for welfare programs as well as the demand on services such as city hospitals.

Urban policy

A large number of planning and policy measures have been developed in recent years to try to meet the growing problems of America's cities. They have formed a constituent component of the New Deal, Fair Deal, New Frontier, Great Society, and New Federalism initiatives of past governments. Until fifty years ago, the precise role of the federal government vis-à-vis the nation's cities was somewhat imprecise because, as the Constitution had not explicitly specified otherwise, the responsibility for cities rested with state governments. The development of an urban policy, however, reflects the increasing recognition that cities are national rather than state assets, and so justify federal aid. An important dilemma with urban policy is that the crisis affects both individuals in cities and urban institutions, so raising questions concerning the balance of aid between people and places. Urban policy in the United States is further complicated by the fragmented structure of local government which gives rise to problems of co-ordination and of the need to ensure that the main beneficiaries of urban programs are those in need, rather than program agencies and their staffs.

The concept of planning was central to the liberal philosophy that inspired Roosevelt's New Deal in the 1930s. It took the form of national and regional initiatives designed to ameliorate the worst effects of the Depression. New Deal recovery policies included federal assistance for both distressed people and for city governments, although the emphasis was on the former. Of particular importance was the income maintenance system created by the 1935 Social Security Act which made provisions for the poor via social insurance and public assistance programs. Alongside, under the Housing Act of 1937, arrangements were made for loans to assist localities in slum clearance and in the building of low rental housing. Another aspect of New Deal policies had more general implications for the city and involved the creation of a National Resources Planning Board to promote planning initiatives at the state level. Many of these initiatives were directed at solving urban problems. Indeed, for Catanese (1979) the Board's two major publications, *Our Cities: Their Role in the National Economy* (1937), and *Urban Planning and Land Policies* (1939), together comprised as much of a national urban policy as the United States ever had. New Deal welfare and housing programs were an important source of aid at the time of acute national economic difficulty, and established the precedent for direct government intervention in the nation's cities.

In the immediate post-war period, such planning as was undertaken by the federal government was primarily oriented towards recovery and the development of the United States economy. The most important urban programs were those concerned with public housing, assistance, and aid as introduced under the National Housing Acts of 1949 and 1954. These strengthened and extended the New Deal slum clearance and urban renewal projects, and encouraged cities to resolve their own problems with federal financial assistance. To ensure that urban renewal and housing schemes were well thought out, the government offered aid through the Section 701 Program which provided matching grants to communities which produced comprehensive plans. Although this arrangement channeled aid directly to the depressed areas of the major cities, the emphasis which was placed upon physical redevelopment meant that comparatively little was accomplished

in social and economic terms. Moreover, as the number of programs proliferated, so the problems of co-ordination and implementation, especially in the nation's larger cities, increased.

These particular deficiencies were redressed somewhat during
the 1960s under President Johnson's "Great Society" initiative by
the War on Poverty, the Economic Opportunity, and the Model
Cities Programs. Whereas the War on Poverty was a general attack
on poverty, and so applied to both urban and rural areas, the
Economic Opportunity and Model Cities Programs were more
specifically urban in direction. The Model Cities Program was
designed to encourage participating cities to develop a concerted
offensive against social and economic problems as well as physical
decay. As outlined in President Johnson's 1966 State of the Union
address, the program "would set in motion the forces of change in
great urban areas that would make them masterpieces of our
civilization." Under the scheme, eligible cities received one-year
planning grants with which to prepare comprehensive plans to
improve the quality of life in their model neighborhoods. Both
implementation and on-going planning would occur over a five-
year demonstration period, during which time funding would be
available through appropriate federal aid programs. Although the
concerted approach was attractive in theory, the program's basic
and broadly stated objectives, which included co-ordinating and
concentrating federal, state, and local resources, developing innovative initiatives, and involving local residents in planning, were
difficult for the cities to define in terms that were locally relevant
and achievable. By the end of 1974, when the program was
eventually abandoned, it had cost an estimated 3 billion dollars
and had turned out to be one of the most unequivocal failures of all
the Great Society initiatives. For Kirwan, the Model Cities Program
epitomized the shortcomings of urban policy in that era:

> ambitious in character, in many ways well conceived, it suffered
> from inadequate funding (especially after the costs of the
> Vietnam war began to mount), from local controversy and
> corruption, and from the inexperience and inability of the
> Federal bureaucracy in the management of so large a program.
> (1981, p. 81)

The Great Society programs were replaced during the 1970s by
the New Federalism system of revenue sharing through which

cities were given blocks of financial aid according to a needs formula. Although originally intended to divert funds away from the major cities, the redistribution mechanisms involved in revenue sharing became the main source of assistance to large central cities during the period of recession after the oil crisis of 1974. This was increased by changes in 1976 to the formula for distribution of the new Community Block Grants to reflect unemployment, the age of housing stock, low rates of population and income growth, and employment losses in manufacturing and retailing. Under the Block Grants, assistance was made available for land acquisition, for the purchase, construction, and renewal of industrial and commercial facilities, for open space and neighborhood facilities, and for planning, housing, rehabilitation, and historic preservation. These measures were supplemented by the Urban Development Action Grants which provided funds to "leverage" private investment in revitalization projects, and assistance was made available under a number of Employment Acts designed to facilitate job creation and training. Together with the major social programs covering assistance to families, medical care, and general measures to promote industry, such as the Small Business Administration Program, they amounted to a comprehensive package of initiatives designed to assist the nation's cities.

Despite the wide range of measures introduced over the past decade, it seems clear that the urban crisis is increasing rather than diminishing in intensity. One reason may lie in the deficiencies of the various initiatives over the years for, as Kirwan (1981) claims, "almost everything has been tried, and nothing has succeeded." He draws attention to the problems of level of funding, the balance of aid to individuals and to institutions, and of co-ordination between federal and local government agencies, that have bedeviled the urban policies of successive administrations. For Kirwan, the shape and evolution of President Carter's urban policy, which was based upon a partnership between federal and city governments, revealed a deep uncertainty, if not actual despair, about the direction that American inner city policy should take. "Nothing in Carter's package represented a radical departure from the thinking of previous administrations, nor did it answer any of the major controversies about the objectives or form of policy" (p. 82).

Some fundamental questions, however, raised in the McGill Commission Report on *Urban America in the Eighties* (Bishop *et al.*,

1980), surround the extent to which urban policy can, indeed should, seek to resolve problems which arise out of the deep-seated social and economic processes which are working against the city. The shifts of population and industry within the post-industrial city, as outlined in the preceding two chapters, are so powerful that they are unlikely to be reversed by planning policy. Equally, as they reflect the locational preferences of the population, it seems reasonable to suppose that they are of general benefit and are likely to lead to the creation of new and higher levels of prosperity. The McGill Commission argued that the near immutability of the technological, economic, social, and demographic trends that herald the emergence of a post-industrial society, and that are responsible for the transformation of the nation's settlements and the life within them, should be recognized and facilitated by policy. Rather than try and retard or reverse the emergence of new economic patterns and relationships, it can be argued that it is the purpose of policy to assist in their creation. For Berry, there are two alternative pathways to constructive change:

> one is for large scale planning that eliminates the central city underclass by income redistribution and renews the cities on a comprehensive basis out of the public purse ... but such a direction is inconsistent with the cultural predispositions and values of the American mainstream. The other is to speed abandonment, to realize that urban civilization without cities. (1975, p. 184)

Accommodating out-migration and urban decline, while relieving the burdens and hardships which fall on those who remain, is the central dilemma for urban policy over the next decade.

5

The agricultural sector

A fundamental change in the role of the agricultural sector is an
integral part of the rise of the post-industrial state. As the emphasis
in the economy shifts away from primary production and manufacturing towards tertiary and quaternary provision, so agriculture
progressively diminishes in importance as a contributor to gross
national product. The contraction of agriculture is indeed a major
indicator of stage in economic development for, unlike the pre-
industrial economy where it is the largest employer, fewer than one
in ten of the labor force in the post-industrial economy is engaged
in food production. This comparative decline, however, masks the
continuing, indeed the increasing, importance of agriculture in
absolute terms. An expanding domestic population with sophisticated and varied eating habits imposes heavy demands upon the
food-producing sector. Moreover, agricultural products are of
strategic importance in a world plagued by shortages and starva-
tion. Although much diminished in relative terms, the agricultural
sector forms a cornerstone of the post-industrial economy.

Despite a major reduction in employment, the agricultural sector
in the United States has proved more than capable of feeding the
rapidly expanding post-war population. Output levels have risen
considerably and consistently so that the United States is not only

self-sufficient in most agricultural products but is a net exporter of many, including strategically important grains and cereals. Over-production rather than shortages is indeed a major problem, necessitating government intervention to regulate prices, buy up surpluses, and reduce the area in agriculture. Increased output has been achieved as a consequence of fundamental and far-reaching shifts in the character of the agricultural sector involving changes in farm structure, organization, and practice. Capital has been sub-stituted for labor in food production so that far fewer people are working larger and more mechanized farms. Applications of science and technology have displaced many traditional customs and techniques resulting in enormous increases in productivity and yield. At the same time, increased emphasis is being placed upon horticulture, dairying, poultry, egg, and beef production, and on the inputs to manufactured foods and food substitutes. Whether these changes amount to what Milk (1972) termed "the new agriculture" is debatable, but they underline the gulf which separates contem-porary agriculture from that at mid-century.

These structural changes have in turn given rise to variations in the spatial pattern of production upon those identified, mapped, and analyzed by Baker (1926). Although the underlying distributions are superficially similar, the increased importance of soybeans, corn, wheat, and rice, and the reduction in the area under tobacco, oats, cotton, and hay, has changed the character of the traditional crop production belts. Moreover, the influence of the market in terms of both the demand for specialized crops and the costs of shipment has altered the pattern at local level. As well as reflecting the influence of different consumption habits, these shifts are strongly linked to the changing size and distribution of the popula-tion. Together they define the agricultural geography of post-industrial America.

Structural changes in agriculture

By any standards, the performance of American agriculture in the post-war period has been most impressive. Despite the very high efficiency of the sector at mid-century, a rise in output has been achieved which has more than kept pace with demand. Moreover, as labor inputs have fallen, this amounts to a major increase in productivity. Based on an index value of 100 for 1967, overall farm output rose by one-third between 1960 and 1980, an increase contributed to in almost equal proportions by livestock and crop production (Table 5.1). All three major categories of livestock products recorded increases, but the 68 per cent growth in poultry and egg output was especially notable. Important differences, however, characterize the performance of the major crops. Food grains, fruits and nuts, and oil crop production rose significantly, whereas the old staples of cotton and tobacco declined. Especially significant in terms of the quantities involved was the increased production of food grains. Output of wheat doubled between 1960 and 1980, and the increase for corn was 60 per cent. Soybean production similarly rose by 64 per cent. The United States can never be completely self-sufficient in food production because it lacks the equatorial environments in which to grow tropical foodstuffs, but agricultural exports in 1980 were twice the value of food, feed, and drink imports.

Table 5.1   *Indices of farm outputs, 1960–80*

1967 = 100

	1960	*1980*	*% change*
Farm Output	91	122	34
Livestock and products	87	113	33
Meat animals	85	111	31
Dairy products	100	110	10
Poultry and eggs	76	128	68
Crops	93	131	41
Feed grains	87	123	41
Hay and forage	90	107	19
Food grains	87	157	80
Vegetables	89	105	18
Fruits and nuts	94	164	75
Sugar	74	114	54
Cotton	196	150	−24
Tobacco	99	90	− 9
Oil	68	171	151

Source: Statistical Abstract of the United States 1981, Table 1212.

The most important feature of post-industrial agriculture is that this increased output has been achieved by a drastically reduced labor force. In 1940 the farm population stood at 31 million, very similar to the numbers for several preceding decades, and comprised 23 per cent of the United States population. The post-war reduction, however, has been so dramatic that the comparable figure for 1980 was 6 million, representing a mere 3 per cent of the total. Those actually employed (as opposed to merely living) on farms similarly fell from 11 million to 4 million over the same period. A reduction in agricultural population and employment is an integral component in the evolution of the post-industrial state as Bell (1973) emphasized, but the scale of contraction and the small size of the sector in the contemporary economy require special emphasis. The most recent statistics indeed suggest that the contraction is continuing. Further substantial job losses in agriculture can be expected as smaller, less efficient, and less profitable farms are absorbed into larger scale operations.

An increase in farm output combined with a much reduced labor force amounts to major gains in agricultural productivity. These are underlined in Table 5.2 which presents some selected indices of farm productivity based upon a value of 100 for 1967. The level of advance necessarily varies according to the type of operation, but the figures for total output per hour point to a fivefold increase over the period. The gain for livestock and products was over sixfold. Nor is this progress diminishing, since the data suggest a quickening pace in recent years. For example, crop production per acre increased by 37 points between 1940 and 1967 (approximately 1.4 points per year) but between 1967 and 1979 it advanced by 29 points (approximately 2.4 points per year). Performance under normal commercial production conditions will never, of course, match the best experimental results, but the existing gaps hold the possibility of further general advance. Record yields for wheat, for example, are 7.7 times those for average United States yields, for sorghums 7.1 times, for soybeans 4.6 times, and for corn 4.3 times (Wittwer, 1975). The achievement appears all the more impressive when compared with that of other sectors of the United States economy which have been unable to match the long-term productivity gains in agriculture. With 1967 as 100, output per man hour in agriculture rose 160 points between 1950 and 1980. In the non-farm sector, the index rose a mere 72 points.

Table 5.2 *Selected indices of farm inputs and productivity, 1950–80*

1967 = 100

	1950	1960	1970	1980
Inputs				
Farm labor	217	145	89	65
Mechanical power and machinery	84	97	100	128
Agricultural chemicals	29	49	115	174
Productivity				
Farm output per hour	34	65	115	194
All livestock and products	37	62	121	240
All crops	36	66	111	165
Cropland used for crops	111	104	98	114

Source: Statistical Abstract of the United States 1981, Tables 1207 and 1211.

The underlying reasons for this increased output and productivity lie not in an expansion of the area under the plow, for the total amount of cropland has remained substantially unchanged since 1950. Instead, it is a consequence of changing farm organization and practices. At its most general level, this amounts to a progressive substitution of capital for labor, with capital inputs per unit of labor input in agriculture increasing from $0.87 in 1910 to $4.00 in 1960 (Heady, Haroldson, Mayer, and Tweeten, 1965). As a consequence, the amount of capital utilized by American agriculture is relatively large. Milk (1972) estimated that in 1970, the level of investment per agricultural worker was about four-and-a-half times the national average amount of capital invested per worker.

Much of the increased investment has been in the application of science and technology to farming. New strains of plants, new breeds of livestock, new kinds of fertilizer, new products and chemical treatments for plant and animal diseases, and improvements in drainage and irrigation techniques together have raised agricultural yields and output. Between 1950 and 1980, the use of agricultural chemicals on the farm increased sixfold suggesting that recent advances in fertilizer and pesticide technology are major factors in agricultural productivity. In 1980, 53 million tons of fertilizer alone were applied to American farms as opposed to 25 million tons in 1960, and the beneficial effects can be seen in

Table 5.3   *Crop and livestock products: yields, 1950–4 to 1975–9*

		Annual average		% change
		1950–4	*1975–9*	
Corn for grain	(bushels per acre)	39.4	95.2	140
Wheat	(bushels per acre)	17.3	31.4	82
Potatoes	(cwt per acre)	151.0	262.0	74
Cotton	(lbs per acre)	296.0	485.0	64
Tobacco	(1000 lbs per acre)	1.3	2.0	54
Milk	(cwt per cow)	54.0	110.0	103

Source: Statistical Abstract of the United States 1981, Table 1213.

improved crop and livestock yields (Table 5.3). Output per unit of all major agricultural products rose significantly between the early 1950s and the late 1970s, and in the case of corn and milk more than doubled.

These advances have been assisted in their practical and economic applications by the development of new machinery, equipment, and techniques. Although the total number of combines, corn pick-ups, balers, and harvesters on the farm did not change appreciably over the period 1950 to 1980, they increased significantly in size and power, as the index of mechanical inputs shows (Table 5.2). The harvesting of grain has been mechanized since McCormick's invention of the reaper in 1847, and Appleby's development of the grain binder (1879), but in the last forty years a range of devices for picking perishable as well as non-perishable crops has been introduced. Examples include an automatic hay baler, a sugar beet harvester, a bean picker, a lettuce cropper, and a tomato combine (Kelly, 1967). These innovations have been complemented by work in genetics which has produced crops which are suitable for mechanized harvesting. For example, a tomato plant has been bred which produces fruit of uniform size that ripen at the same time and that are strong enough to withstand mechanical handling (Webb and Bruce, 1968). Within five years of the introduction of the combine and the improved fruit in 1962, about 80 per cent of tomatoes grown in the United States for processing were harvested by machine. Although many of these developments involve minor crops, these crops are among the most labor-intensive and so the effects of mechanization upon employment levels have been especially pronounced. Other than soft fruits, most grain, legume, root, tuber, vine, and stemcrops are now harvested mechanically.

Advances in water supply and use have contributed to agricultural productivity in particular regions of the United States. Not only has irrigation extended the area capable of sustained cultivation but it has raised yields in existing farm areas. In 1950, total irrigated areas measured some 10.1 million hectares (25 million acres) and in 1980, 18.2 million hectares (45 million acres). As almost all of this increase occurred in the arid South-West where temperature and length of growing season are highly favorable to agriculture, the effect on output was especially pronounced. The combined contributions of science and technology enable fewer and fewer American farmers to continually produce more food from the same amount of land.

The organization of farming

The further refinement of advanced farming techniques has been assisted by the move towards larger producing units. Between 1940 and 1980, the number of farms fell from 6.4 million to 2.4 million, resulting in an increase in the average size of farm from 67.5 to 173.7 hectares (167 to 430 acres). Variations in size, however, remain wide, and it is important to note that farms of over 404 hectares (1000 acres), which number 7 per cent of all farms, account for 59 per cent of all land in farms. Equally important are variations across the states which reflect differences in types of farming, land productivity, and historical development. Large farms predominate in the West where average farm sizes in the Dakotas, Montana, Wyoming, Colorado, New Mexico, and Nevada are in excess of 404 hectares (1000 acres). Elsewhere, farms are very much smaller, the average for the North-East, North Central and South regions lying between 68.7 and 145.4 hectares (170 to 360 acres).

In a detailed survey of changes in farming in the Willamette Valley, Oregon, Van Otten (1980) found that the mean size of farms had increased from 126 hectares (313 acres) to 176 hectares (424 acres) between 1946 and 1976. Of the reasons for change cited by a sample of farmers, economies of scale was the most important, and accounted for 38 per cent of responses. As farmers have mechanized their operations and become more market-oriented, the fixed costs associated with agricultural production have become important. In striving for optimal efficiency, farm operators have generally enlarged their land bases to spread total fixed costs over larger production units. Van Otten also noted that failure to make size adjustments consistent with increasing fixed costs of production led to the economic failure of some farms. Other reasons given for changes in farm size included the desire to obtain land with a particular set of characteristics, the proximity of available land to the headquarters farm, the need for water, land speculation, and inheritance.

One consequence of the increased demand for farmland is that operators have rented and leased land which is not contiguous to the headquarters farm, so that farms have become more geographically dispersed. The growth of fragmented farms was noted by Van Otten in the Willamette Valley, but it is a nationwide trend. Indeed, it is the norm in large parts of Minnesota, where many farms consist of six or seven tracts of land, as Smith (1975) has observed. Because of the fragmentation of their holdings, farmers are not able to benefit fully from economies of scale, as costs in time and money are incurred in moving themselves, their implements, and their stock from tract to tract. Many farmers have become commuters on their own farms. Fragmentation of farms also has important social consequences for, by separating the farmer from his land, it undermines the basis for community life in rural America.

A second product of increases in farm size is the rise in farm land values. Although they have moved consistently upward since the Depression, the increase during the 1970s, when land values more than doubled, was unprecedented. An element of speculation is a contributory factor, but the underlying reasons are the pressures towards farm enlargement that produce demand-led inflation. Paradoxically, it is the large-scale farmer who benefits most from this trend, as the rising value of the farm enables him to raise a larger mortgage to buy or rent more land and, with increased economies of scale, to engage in more profitable production. Small and medium sized farms which are unincorporated are disadvantaged, especially when the farmer dies. The need to pay inheritance taxes, which are based upon current farm values, is an increasing cause of agricultural indebtedness. In more extreme cases it may be necessary to sell the farm, so reinforcing the general trend towards larger scale units.

The increase in farm size is, however, only one facet of the change in scale which also involves a growth in the size of turnover. For example, between 1969 and 1978, the number of farms with annual sales of $100,000 or more rose from 3 to 12 per cent. Such increases typically result from a greater intensity of operation on units of all sizes and so affect farms across the nation, as Gregor (1982) has shown. Whether measured in terms of geographical area or value of output, the trend towards larger scale operation is one of the most pronounced trends in contemporary United States agriculture.

Increases in farm size and turnover are in part associated with the growing influence and control which big business exercises over agriculture. At its most general level, this involves the decline in family farming and the growth in the number of incorporated farming operations. The latter stood at about 8 per cent of all farms in 1978. Incorporation provides a means of increasing the capitalization of the unit so enabling the farmer to enjoy higher economies of scale. It is also, however, frequently undertaken by family farmers as a means of protecting their investments and writing off tax losses incurred elsewhere, rather than as an aid to increased farm profitability. These very different motives tend to obscure the extent and significance of incorporation. Depending upon how the statistics and trends are interpreted, the decline in family farming can be seen as either "a myth" (Wheeler and Muller, 1981) or else "a serious threat to rural traditions" (Gregor, 1982).

A more significant trend associated with both increased scale of operation and change of ownership is the extension to agriculture of the vertical integration linkages traditionally associated with manufacturing processes. For a variety of reasons, large corporations in the past avoided the production side of agriculture and concentrated on providing inputs of machinery, fertilizers, pesticides, and feeds; and the outputs of the processing, packaging and marketing of food products. One reason for this was that profits were not in general to be found in agricultural production, another was the price of prime agricultural land, while a third was that farming was poorly suited to centralized management. As a consequence, agricultural machinery, agricultural chemical, canning, and freezing companies were household names, but farming operators were not. Economies of vertical integration "from the seed to the supermarket" are now such that farming is being added progressively to the activities of large corporations. The availability of food products in the right quantity, at the right time and at the right price is best assured if the company controls every stage of the supply process. The term "agribusiness" has been coined to denote large industrial type operations along the commercial food chain.

Although the precise contribution of agribusiness to current agricultural production, thought to be in the region of 10 per cent, is unclear, there is no doubt that it is growing rapidly. Moreover, its presence appears pronounced because it is concentrated in specific specialized sectors including broiler, seed, vegetable, citrus, feed cattle, turkey, and egg production (Walsh, 1975). In a detailed study of corporate farming in California, Dorel (1975), reported by Parsons (1977), traced the growth of agribusiness. In California in 1969, 2000 farm corporations, including incorporated family farms, owned or controlled 15 per cent of commercial cropland and accounted for half of all farm products sold. They were responsible for the production of about 90 per cent of the state's melons, two-thirds of its lettuce, 40 per cent of its cotton, and one-third of its nuts, carrots, and potatoes. The nature and scale of operations involved is illustrated by Tenneco Inc., a Houston based conglomerate. In 1969 it owned 52,520 hectares (130,000 acres) of prime farmland in California as a result of the acquisition of a land company, and also a major farm machinery manufacturer, a carton manufacturer, and the nation's leading processor and shipper of fruits, nuts, and fresh vegetables. Subdivisions of the corporation had major shopping center interests in San Joaquin Valley cities. With this scale of operation, the company controlled and profited from all aspects of the food chain, from production to consumption. Moreover, as large amounts of produce were derived from non-company farmers working under contract, the corporation was in a position to retrench with minimal losses if markets weakened.

A second example of agribusiness is the production of chicken broilers. This type of poultry raising has always been strongly market-oriented on account of the weight loss and perishability of freshly killed birds, and one of its major concentrations is in the Delmarva Peninsula, close to the cities of Megalopolis. In studying this area, Hart (1975) found that broiler production is now dependent upon sophisticated management techniques and factory-like methods. Whereas more than two hundred small companies controlled production in the Peninsula in 1945, only ten remain, and all are structured around high volume scale economies. Assembly line manufacturing complete with conveyor belts dominates, and rapid turnovers are assured by the fact that the latest breed of broiler requires only seven weeks from hatching to maturity. Highly scientific procedures are widespread: chicken diets are fully computerized and complex drugs are used routinely both to prevent disease and to accelerate growth. Increased vertical integration has removed much of the control of the operation from farmers, who supply buildings and labor but are provided with chicks and feed by outside managers, in return for the security of a guaranteed price. Hart cites the example of Perdue Inc. of Salisbury (Maryland), a company which markets 1.6 million broilers, supplied by 800 Delmarva farmers, each week. Perdue orchestrates the entire production cycle from hatchery through processing and marketing, and owns its own feed mills and genetic research facilities. This type of operation is typical of that in broiler production and is indicative of the scale and character of operation that is involved in modern agribusiness.

Despite its contribution to increased output, the growth of agribusiness has not been without its critics. One set of fears is environmental for, under large-scale corporate farming, land is reduced to a commodity which is bought, sold, cropped, or subdivided to maximize short-term gain. There is little place for agricultural practices which are designed to maintain soil fertility and productivity in the long term. Others have drawn attention to the adverse consequences of impersonal and distant agribusiness for traditional ways of life in rural America. In several Mid-Western states, corporate farming has been either outlawed or sharply restricted (Parsons, 1977). The continuing growth of agribusiness in other regions suggests, however, that it will play an increasingly important role in the agriculture of post-industrial America.

Agriculture and the federal government

As well as changes taking place on the farm, the character of post-war agriculture has been profoundly affected by policies of the federal government. Federal intervention in the agricultural sector has increased significantly over the last forty years as evidenced by the scale of direct government payments to farmers. In 1950, the federal commitment stood at a third of a billion dollars, but by 1980 it had risen to nearly 5 billion. The proportion of farmers' net incomes which this represents rose from 2 per cent to about 25 per cent over the same period. However, as much expenditure takes the form of support payments which are linked to the size of the harvest, federal outlays do vary markedly from year to year. Thus agricultural expenditure in 1977 was twice that in 1976 but two-thirds of the 1978 figure.

Federal expenditure is designed to deal with the complex set of difficulties that beset American agriculture on account of its distinctive supply and demand circumstances. On the supply side, American farmers throughout the post-war period have kept production well in excess of demand which has depressed prices and restricted farmers' incomes. A consequent problem has been how to reduce and dispose of agricultural surpluses. At the same time, per capita incomes across the nation have risen to a level at which domestic demand has become highly inelastic. In 1980, the average American consumer spent only 16 per cent of disposable income on agricultural produce and, as the consumer was able to buy all the food needed, a further increase in income has little effect on food consumption (Heady, 1976). Farmers' problems have been further exacerbated by the conflicts generated by contemporary science which is helping to increase agricultural output while at the same time exhorting the consumer to reduce total food intake, switch to low calorie, low fat products, and to stop smoking. To say that American farmers have been too successful for their own good may be simplistic, but it is close to the truth. Post-war advances in agricultural output have made food a commodity that is in abundance rather than shortage, to the detriment of the farmers' financial position.

Contemporary agricultural policy traces its origins to the Depression of the 1930s, and the attempts at amelioration introduced as part of Roosevelt's New Deal. To counteract the collapse in agricultural prices, the government passed the Agricultural Adjustment Act of 1933 under which farmers were paid to reduce their planted acreage and output. They were also loaned money and storage facilities in such a way that the rate at which their products were released on the market was controlled. The program was administered by the Commodity Credit Corporation which was created with the aim of stabilizing, supporting, and protecting farm incomes and prices, assisting in the maintenance of balanced adequate supplies of agricultural commodities, and facilitating the orderly distribution of agricultural goods. The Corporation was empowered to buy, store, and sell farm commodities, and to make cash advances to farmers for their products before the harvest. Alongside these measures aimed at regulating the domestic market, international food-aid schemes were devised to subsidize exports, which in some cases amounted to actually giving produce away. A second Adjustment Act was passed in 1938, which provided for mandatory price support for stipulated crops (initially corn, wheat, and cotton), and for marketing quotas for these and other commodities.

The paradox with agricultural policy at mid-century was that, while the adjustment programs sought to reduce the level of agricultural production, the effect of federal government expenditure on agricultural research, soil conservation, and irrigation was to increase it. Indeed, as agriculture continued to improve its technology, the programs controlling the supply of food to the market served only to slow the growth of farm output, not to stop it. As government supply control programs curtailed the areas planted to crops, so farmers cultivated the land more intensively and applied even greater quantities of fertilizer and pesticides. In consequence, surpluses accumulated throughout the 1950s and 1960s, and the Commodity Credit Corporation continued in operation, using its powers to support numerous farm products. These, most notably and consistently, were wheat, corn, rice, cotton, and tobacco.

The fight against surpluses up to 1972 was supplemented by various additional attempts to reduce the farmed area. For example, the Agricultural Act of 1956 established a "soil bank" scheme under which farmers were paid for taking land out of crops in surplus supply and placing it in the bank. At its peak in 1957, about 8.5 million hectares (21 million acres) were in the "bank" but as farmers deposited their poorest land and continued to cultivate their remaining areas more intensively, outputs continued to rise. In consequence, this scheme was abolished in 1958. Attempts to persuade farmers to retire land continued, however, under the Emergency Feed Grains Program of 1961 and the Cropland Adjustment Program of 1966 (Estall, 1972). The former aimed to retire land out of corn, sorghums, barley, and oats, offering considerable financial incentives; the latter had many similarities to the earlier soil bank scheme but provided only for long terms of retirement (5–10 years), and offered less inducement. Estall estimates that under these various schemes, the total diverted area amounted to 10.1 million hectares (25 million acres) in 1961, rose erratically to 28.9 million hectares (62 million acres) in 1972, and subsequently dropped sharply as domestic circumstances changed.

In parallel with these restrictions on production, attempts were also made to stimulate demand in both domestic and foreign markets. At home, the Commodity Credit Corporation arranged to dispose of food surpluses via programs of aid to needy sections of the American population. The school lunch program, the food stamp scheme (by which the poor purchased food to several times the value of the food stamp they bought), and direct distribution of free food to the poorest families, are all examples of welfare schemes which also benefited agriculture. Similarly, exports of feed grains, rice, tobacco and milk under foreign food aid programs were maintained at a high level throughout the 1950s and 1960s. For example, more than one-fifth of all wheat grown in the United States was exported in 1965 and more than a fourth in 1970. Wheat exports more than doubled between 1971 and 1972 in response to the failure of the Russian wheat harvest.

For Estall (1972), the successes of United States agricultural policy up to the early 1970s were threefold. The first was that it "brought unusual stability to total farm income" and the second that it "cushioned the impact of large shifts in demand and supply relationships by giving more time for adjustment." The third was that "it provided some insurance for national and international emergencies" (p.162). On the debit side, the schemes were expensive, and as primary emphasis was placed upon the land, little attention was paid to long-term social and economic effects. Implications for the structure of farming were especially far-reaching as the subsidies benefited the largest, most efficient units the most. Conversely, many marginal farming operations, which were dependent on federal payments to stay in business, collapsed when they were withdrawn.

The supply control programs were eliminated by the 1972 Agriculture and Consumer Protection Act which left farmers free to make their own decisions about what to grow. In their place the federal government now provides a safety net in the form of deficiency payments which are made if free market prices fall below set "target" levels. In practice, the extent of federal involvement has been lower in recent years because the 1970s was a decade of relative security and prosperity for the American farmer. The most important change was the growth in world markets for agricultural produce, especially in Third World and Eastern Bloc countries, which American farmers were well placed to exploit: the value of agricultural exports increased fivefold between 1970 and 1980. Although helping to reduce surpluses, however, this meant that agricultural products increased in strategic importance, as President Carter's Russian grain embargo of 1979 emphasized. The prosperity of American agriculture is as likely to be determined by foreign policy in the future as it was by price support and acreage control provisions in the past.

The changing geography of agriculture

The effects of structural change in agriculture and increased federal government involvement are seen in the spatial patterns of crop production that define the agricultural geography of modern America (Figure 5.1). Maps for each major commodity outline the broad regional patterns of agricultural activity and identify distributional relationships which reflect both environmental and economic constraints. The climatic and soil requirements of some crops mean that they are restricted to comparatively small areas across the nation while the incidence of those that thrive under a wider range of conditions is determined primarily by economic considerations. Similarly, at a local scale the combined influence of physical and economic factors is critical. For example, the distribution of cotton-producing areas within the South-East is a product of both edaphic and socio-economic circumstances as Hart (1978) has shown.

The locational principles of Thunen, expounded in 1826, go some way towards explaining the economic factors that determine the distribution of individual crops. The basic premise in Thunen's approach was that decisions as to which crop to grow where

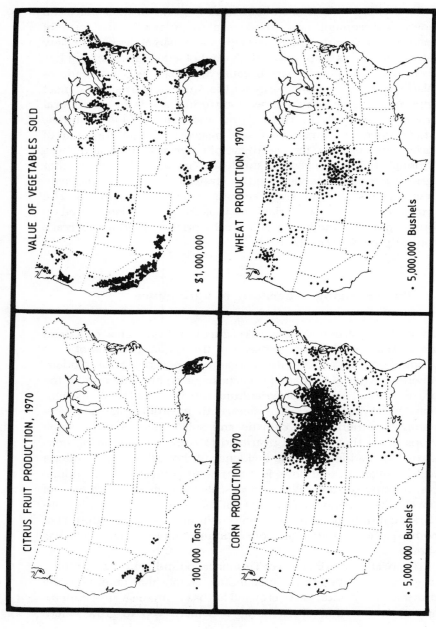

Figure 5.1 · *The distribution of agricultural production*

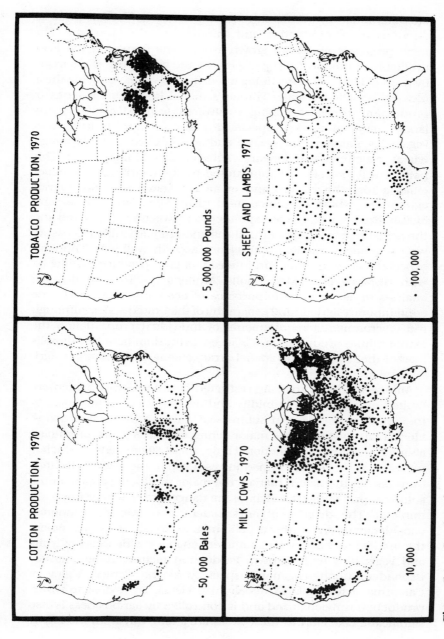

Figure 5.1   Continued

are determined by profitability which is a function of sale price at, minus costs of production and shipment to, the farm gate. The most profitable crops are grown around the farm, and the least profitable in the most distant fields, so the farmhouse is encircled by rings of land use of declining intensity and value. Applying these ideas at a national scale, Thunen's model postulates a series of production zones stretching westwards from Megalopolis, the largest national market, specializing successively in fruits and vegetables, dairying, mixed crop and livestock "corn belt farming," wheat, ranching, and forestry (Wheeler and Muller, 1981). This pattern will, however, be interrupted by the distribution of major cities across the nation, and of areas of superior and inferior agriculture, which introduce local distortions. For Wheeler and Muller, there is a close correspondence between the predicted and the actual pattern of agricultural activities. In particular, the east to west sequence of agricultural regions accords well with Thunen's expectations, with value and intensity of crop produced falling off with distance from Megalopolis. Muller's (1973) more detailed analysis underlines the importance of economic distance in the contemporary agricultural geography of the United States. Although the environmental requirements of individual crops define the extreme limits of cultivation, it is access to the dominant Megalopolis market that dictates the spatial arrangement of the nation's agricultural systems.

Among the most spatially restricted are those crops which are limited on account of humidity and temperature requirements to the "mediterranean" and subtropical areas of the United States. Florida has long been the major center for citrus fruits, producing about three-fifths of the national crop, about 80 per cent of which is marketed as frozen or canned juices. Despite the greater distance from the North-Eastern market, the major producing area is in the southern part of the state where the dangers from winter frosts are minimal. The dictates of environment also override economic considerations in southern California, Arizona, and Texas where the mild winters and warm summers enable a wide range of fruits and vegetables to be grown. Production techniques are heavily dependent upon irrigation, especially in the Central Valley of California, resulting in extremely high yields. The extent to which production is mechanized and is controlled by agribusiness is also significant. Like Florida, these areas are a long way from the highly

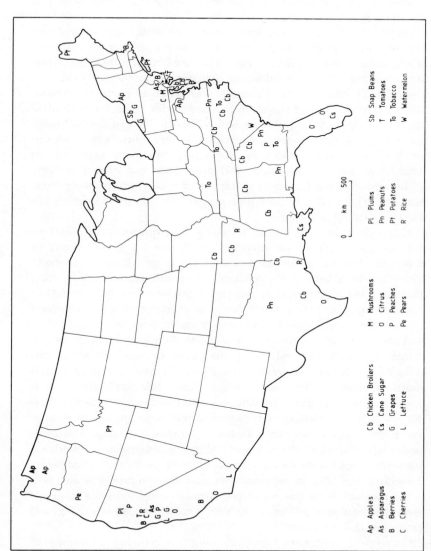

Figure 5.2   *Agricultural specialty areas*

populated North-East and so many fruit and vegetable products are canned, frozen, or otherwise processed before being dispatched to the market.

Since mid-century, there have been many shifts and relocations of fruit and vegetable production in California so that the patterns of specialization identified in Figure 5.2 are both highly generalized and transitory. The advantage of irrigation is such that fruit and vegetable production has generally moved away from the coastal and southern areas of the state to the interior so that the Central Valley comprises a complex mosaic of highly localized and highly specialized producing areas. California is the foremost state for the production of fruit and vegetables. It is the only state where honeydew melons, almonds, and artichokes are grown on any scale, and it is the foremost producer of some twenty other fruit, nut, and vegetable crops of which grapes, lettuce, and tomatoes are the most valuable by far.

Although limited in overall terms by environment, the distribution of the other crops mapped in Figure 5.1 owes much to economic factors. Particularly significant is proximity to markets which is critical for highly perishable commodities, so dairy farming and the production of fresh vegetables are heavily concentrated in the densely populated North-East. Most major cities are indeed surrounded by milksheds and market gardens as Gottmann (1961) and Durand (1964) noted. Financial considerations account for the distribution of wheat and corn production, for although wheat can be grown with great success in the Mid-West, as the extremely high yields in Illinois, Indiana, Missouri, and Michigan show, it is displaced by corn, the more valuable and the more productive crop (Figure 5.1). As a consequence, wheat is the more important crop in the High Plains states of the Dakotas, Kansas, Nebraska, Montana, and the panhandles of Texas and Oklahoma, where lower yields on account of less favorable climatic conditions are more than offset by the enormous acreage planted. Distance from markets is also less critical as wheat is the more transferable crop, both in terms of lower movement costs and the ability to withstand handling and long periods of storage.

Differences of climate, especially length of growing season, mean that spring wheat is the dominant crop in the Dakotas and Montana, while higher yielding winter wheat is raised in the southern High Plains. Although the Plains have long been regarded as an area of monoculture, the traditional wheat-fallow rotation in the winter wheat areas has been supplemented over the last thirty years by the addition of grain sorghums as a feed crop. In part, this is a response to the uncertainties associated with wheat, which is the crop most commonly in surplus over the post-war period. One reason for continued overproduction is the marginal nature of High Plains environments which has always encouraged overplanting to reduce risks. A second is the high level of price support for wheat under federal agricultural policies, which encouraged farmers to go on growing it when in some cases they would have been wiser to put down their land to grazing. A third is the need to expand rather than to reduce the area under cultivation in order to derive the maximum economies of scale from mechanization. In other responses to the uncertainties associated with wheat growing, farmers have diversified, either by spreading their interests across the wheat belt, or by developing sources of income outside agriculture. For example, in suitcase farming, farmers live some distance away from their farms or, owning farms in different parts of the plains, migrate between them on a seasonal basis. Similarly, on the margins of the wheat-growing areas, the practice of sidewalk farming, in which the operator lives in a local town where he also has a part-time job, has also been recognized (Kollmorgan and Jenks, 1958a, 1958b).

Superimposing the individual patterns in Figure 5.1 and adding the major areas of specialization in other crops is necessarily a highly subjective exercise, but it produces a useful map of overall agricultural activity. Despite half a century of change in farming, Figure 5.3 suggests that the concept of crop belts has considerable continuing relevance in American agriculture. Winsberg (1980) indeed has shown that sales of several leading agricultural commodities including cattle and calves, fruit and nuts, nursery products, Irish potatoes, peanuts, sheep, wool, vegetables, and wheat, were more geographically concentrated in the late 1970s than they were in 1939, so the belts are of greater importance. Rather than breaking down under the impact of universally available science and technology, and the rapid innovation and diffusion of new ideas, increased geographical specialization is a major feature of post-war agriculture.

Such changes as have occurred since mid-century involve the characteristics of agriculture at the intra-regional rather than the inter-regional scale. Two differences merit particular comment. The

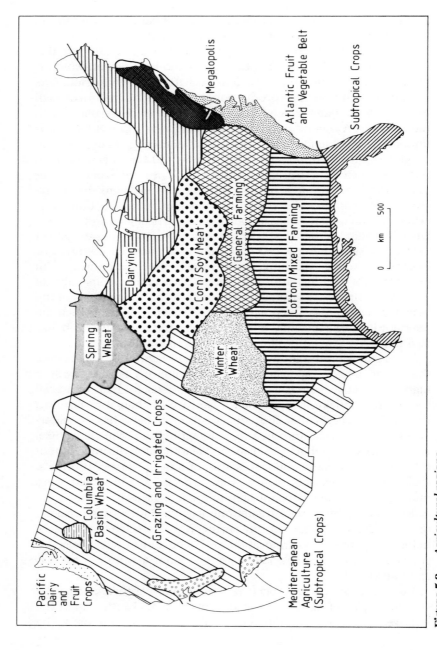

Figure 5.3   *Agricultural regions*

first is the contraction of the area under cotton and its implications for agriculture in the cotton belt; the second is the changing character of the corn belt as a consequence of new crop combinations and the increased importance of soybean production. An examination of these changes in detail shows the ways in which shifts have occurred in the spatial patterns of food production in response to structural changes, and federal government involvement, in agriculture.

Some spatial trends in agriculture

A decline in the area under cotton is one of the most pronounced features of post-war American agriculture. Very nearly 14.5 million hectares (36 million acres) were given over to cotton in 1940, but in 1980, the figure was 5.2 million hectares (13 million acres). The effects of this reduction were, however, only partly offset by increases in yields, as the 24 per cent fall in cotton output over the period 1960–80 shows (Table 5.1). Associated with this overall decline are some important regional shifts in cotton production. Though never exclusive to the area, cotton was traditionally a South-Eastern crop to the extent that the six states of Arkansas, Louisiana, Mississippi, Alabama, South Carolina, and Georgia produced 53 per cent of United States cotton in 1940 (Hart, 1967). At the time, 28 per cent of the cropland in these states was planted to cotton, making it the most important crop. Today, an area in the South-West, stretching west from the Texas and Oklahoma panhandles through southern New Mexico and Arizona into the San Joaquin Valley of California, is the leading area, contributing about 65 per cent of total production (Figure 5.1). Texas, a state which straddles the divide between South-East and South-West is the leading producer, with California a poor second. Yield per unit area in the South-Western states of Arizona and California far exceeds that in South-Eastern producing areas (Table 5.4).

These changes in the distribution of cotton production reflect the combined effects of government policy and response to new technology. A trend away from cotton was encouraged after 1933 under the Agricultural Adjustment Act, which instituted cotton price supports and crop controls. The aim was to drive up prices and curtail overproduction. One response among South-Eastern farmers was to concentrate cotton on the best land, cultivating

Table 5.4 **Cotton: area harvested and yield by state, 1980**

State	Acreage harvested (000s)	Yield per acre (lb)
Texas	6873	234
California	1500	995
Mississippi	1125	488
Arkansas	645	330
Arizona	631	1085
Oklahoma	565	174
Louisiana	560	390
Alabama	321	411

Source: Statistical Abstract of the United States 1981, Table 1231.

more intensively to increase yields, but this was not a viable strategy for many small operators, so they ceased cotton production. In consequence, cotton continued its long-term trend of a reduction in the area under cultivation in the South-East, as mapped by Prunty (1951) and Hart (1967).

Although federal government policies may have contributed to the reduction in the area under cotton, they were applied to all areas and so were not primarily responsible for inter-regional shifts in cotton production. Instead, the rate of adoption of new practices and technology was critical. In a detailed study of the disintegration of cotton growing in the Appalachian Piedmont, Prunty and Aiken (1972) considered a number of contributory factors. The ravages of the boll weevil were especially serious in the inter-war period but by 1940 cotton production had largely recovered its lost ground. Similarly, the decline of plantation farming and of share-cropping were seen to be of historical rather than contemporary importance. For Prunty and Aiken, a viable cotton-growing complex existed in the Piedmont until the 1950s. Its essential characteristics were the large number of small allotment farmers involved, hand picking of the crop, and the intensive nature of production which necessitated large labor inputs in seedbed preparation, planting, thinning, weeding, and harvesting. Although a mechanized and relatively low cost production technology for picking the fiber had been available for thirty years, few producers in the Piedmont adopted it. There was a lack of appreciation of the benefits of mechanization and an unwillingness to form the multiple tenancies through which small allotments could be profitable under new technology. Similarly, few ginning machines, which could process mechanically picked cotton, were in use in the area. In contrast, cotton was being grown increasingly in the South-West in large-scale capital intensive and highly mechanized operations. Environmental conditions, especially the timing and length of the harvesting period, were more conducive to mechanization, and South-Western growers were able to produce a low cost, high quality product. The consequence was that the position of the Piedmont cotton growers became increasingly more marginal and unprofitable. The experiences in the Piedmont were not necessarily repeated exactly across the South-East because production conditions differed, but they were replicated in general. Cotton production fell because South-Eastern producers were either unwilling or unable to change their traditional practices so as to make use of new technology. Given the opportunity to grow alternative crops, and faced with competition from producers elsewhere, they moved out of cotton altogether.

Within the South-East, cotton growing has contracted to those areas in which the most fertile soils ensure the highest yields and so the best chances of competition. In the most important area, which stretches south from the Ohio confluence to New Orleans, cotton is grown in the rich alluvial soils which lie between the Mississippi and its tributaries, the Yazoo and the Red River. A second area is in northern Alabama, while a third comprises a string of scattered "islands" within the Appalachian Piedmont that constitute all that remain of a previously highly prosperous cotton-growing region (Prunty and Aiken, 1972). Cotton production in eastern Texas is concentrated in the Black Prairie ("Black Waxie") soil areas and along the coastal strip including the lower valley of the Rio Grande. These areas are quite separate from the Texas high plain and panhandle areas where cotton is grown under irrigation.

The dramatic decline in the importance of cotton is only one element in the changing pattern of crop production in the South. Between 1939 and 1974 the area under the five traditional southern cash crops of cotton, rice, cane sugar, tobacco, and peanuts was more than halved by a fall of 3.2 million hectares (8 million acres), (Hart, 1978). The area under rice tripled, but the area devoted to cotton, tobacco, and especially peanuts dropped sharply. The loss, however, was offset by an increase of nearly 4.0 million hectares (10 million acres) under soybeans which effectively replaced corn as the principal field crop of the South. Although the existence of specialty crop-producing areas in the South has long been recognized, these changes in the extent of cultivation altered their prominence in the agricultural landscape. As exemplified by cotton, and for very similar reasons, the major cash crops all became more concentrated in distinctive "island" regions which offered the best geological, edaphic, and climatic conditions (Hart, 1978).

The most important corollary of this increasing concentration was the wholesale abandonment of cropland in the South to brush and forest. As crops became more concentrated in the most favorable locations, so vast areas of poor land were left to decline. Hart's statistics underline the magnitude of this change by showing that the total area of cropland harvested in the ten Southern states fell from 23.8 million hectares (59 million acres) in 1939, to 15.3 million hectares (38 million acres) in 1974. Within states, many counties lost three-quarters of their harvested cropland over the period. Although government programs that were designed to release marginal land from production may have played a minor part, the reasons for abandonment were primarily environmental. Hart's analysis showed that the areas of greatest cropland loss suffered from major environmental limitations, such as steep slopes and poor, infertile soils, that severely constrain the types of operation in which farmers can successfully engage. The introduction of post-industrial science and technology, especially new forms of mechanized production, into an area with a highly varied physical environment imposed a new pattern on the agricultural geography of the South. Areas that were best placed to exploit the advantages of mechanization increased in importance as centers of production. Areas which were marginal were abandoned.

The introduction of new crops and farming practices has also altered the character of O.E. Baker's corn belt since mid-century. Despite giving its name to the region, corn was never the only crop grown. Rather, it formed part of a triangular feed crop rotation, with small grains and hay, the products of which were marketed "on the hoof" as high quality pork and beef. As livestock sales regularly accounted for three-quarters of farmers' incomes, the labels "meat belt" or "corn–meat belt" were more accurate. Within the area, the types of grains grown in association with corn varied widely as

Weaver (1954) observed, so that the belt could also be seen as a set of crop combination regions with corn as the common denominator. Although the generally mixed character of farming remains, the increase in the area under soybeans and the simplification of crop rotations have changed the emphasis in local production. Corn belt agriculture today is oriented towards corn, soybean, and meat production.

The most important changes in the agriculture of the area follow from the introduction of soybeans in place of small grains in the traditional cropping pattern. The soybean is a comparatively new crop to the United States, and before 1929 was grown on too restricted a basis to justify the publication of production figures in the Census of Agriculture (Hart, 1972). For this reason, soybeans were never subject to the post-New Deal quotas and limitations and, in consequence, cultivation and output rose dramatically. A fourfold increase in production was recorded between 1960 and 1980 alone. To the farmer, the main advantages of soybean production stem from its versatility. It is eminently suited to environmental conditions in the Mid-West where, used in rotation, its soil-enriching properties mean that extensive areas can be cropped for long periods under highly profitable corn. Moreover, it can be sold as a high protein food, a valuable source of vegetable oil, or as an ingredient in a wide range of edible products from milk substitutes to meat extenders. It also has important industrial applications in the manufacture of plastics, lubricants, antifreezes, and paints. For these reasons, soybeans have displaced small grains in the traditional triangular rotation and have become the second ranking crop in terms of farm value in every state of the central corn belt.

The introduction of soybean production has underlined and reinforced the position of the Mid-West as the premier agricultural region in the nation. California and Texas are the leading states in terms of total value of farm products sold, but the contribution of the corn–soy–meat belt states of Iowa, Illinois, Indiana, and Ohio is underlined when the figures are adjusted to take account of variations in the size of states. Only Delaware with its highly intensive poultry farming industry produces a more valuable agricultural product per unit area (Table 5.5). The primacy of the corn–soy–meat belt stems in part from its natural advantages of flat land, rich soils, and warm humid summers which are conducive to high productivity, but it also owes much to the system of agricul-

Table 5.5   *Sales of farm products by leading states, 1978*

State	Farm sales (million dollars)	
	Total	Per square mile
Delaware	325	0.16
Iowa	8193	0.15
Illinois	5914	0.10
Indiana	3354	0.09
Maryland	799	0.08
Ohio	2842	0.07
Nebraska	5152	0.07
Wisconsin	3449	0.06
Kansas	4996	0.06
California	9284	0.06

Source: Statistical Abstract of the United States 1981, Table 1175.

ture which has developed in the region. Mid-Western farms are large, capital intensive, and highly modernized, and Mid-Western farmers are among the most progressive and innovative in the nation. New agricultural technologies and practices diffuse rapidly through the area, and are adopted rapidly if they offer an improvement in operating efficiency and output (Brown, 1980). Information flows are crucial to this process of innovation and change, and the corn–soy–meat belt farmers are served by an exceptional network of agricultural communications.

The most important source of information is via technical journals directed at the farming community. In 1970, the Mid-West was the leading region for agricultural publishing, with 157 of the 386 farm magazines analyzed by Evans and Salcedo (1974) being produced in the area. According to Brunn and Raitz's (1978) list of farm magazines, 114, or 30 per cent of the national total, were published in the eight Mid-West states in 1977. Although a large number were produced in and around Minneapolis–St Paul, Chicago, and Kansas City, farm magazine publishing was undertaken in 73 towns and cities in the area, thereby ensuring a high level of accessibility to farmers across the region. Another feature was the large number of highly specialized magazines geared to the needs of specific types of agriculture which were published in the region. As well as articles on farming, magazines provide a medium through which implement manufacturers, seed companies, and pesticide and insecticide firms can advertise their products, and the government can publicize the results of agricultural research work. The combined effect of natural advantages and advanced production systems made possible by the rapid and widespread knowledge and use of the most recent developments in science and technology explains the success of Mid-Western agriculture specifically, and of American farming in general.

Conclusion

In common with manufacturing industry, the agricultural sector has undergone a comprehensive restructuring over the post-war period. An increase in the scale of farming, as indicated by the rise in average farm sizes, and the progressive replacement of capital for labor, which has reduced the level of agricultural employment, are two indices of this change. The third is the growth of agribusinesses in which agricultural production is subsumed within vertically integrated, industrial types of operation which are responsible for all stages of food production "from seed to supermarket." Together, these organizational changes have contributed to major increases in agricultural output and productivity which have generated sizable food surpluses despite rising demand as a consequence of population increase over the post-war period. As important, however, has been the mechanization of agriculture, and the increased use of improved strains, fertilizers, and pest controls. Soil and climatic inputs alone no longer explain the productivity of American agriculture. High output is due as much to the appliction of post-industrial organizational techniques, science, and technology.

Despite these structural changes, the pattern of agricultural activity across the nation today is broadly similar to that recognized by Baker (1926), over fifty years ago. Areas of specialization, determined by a combination of environmental and economic factors, remain, and the concept of crop and crop combination belts is still central to the understanding of the geography of agriculture. Such changes as have occurred involve shifts in the emphasis of production within the belts, involving variations in the importance of individual crops, as the examples of agricultural trends in the

South-East and the Mid-West show. The reduction in the area under cotton, and the rise in importance of soybeans are detailed examples of the general responses of farmers to the changing economics of crop production which follow from developments in agricultural organization and technology. The progression into post-industrialism has yet to transform the pattern overall, but it is responsible for a set of subtle shifts in the agricultural geography of the United States at the local scale.

6

Distributional problems and policies

A recurring theme over the preceding five chapters has been the extraordinary richness of contemporary America. In comparison with many other advanced and developed nations, the United States enjoys a range of climatic and soil types conducive to varied and successful agriculture, a highly favorable population: resource ratio, and leadership in most areas of science and technology. The workforce is highly educated, adaptive, and innovative, and the population can expect to stay healthy and live as long as the residents of most other nations. Despite cyclical fluctuations, the economy over the past forty years has remained buoyant, generating high levels of output and sustaining near to full employment. In consequence, the considerable affluence enjoyed at mid-century has been further and substantially increased over the post-war period.

Although the richness of contemporary America is a source of considerable envy, many have criticized the socio-economic system for failing to spread the benefits of post-industrial affluence more equitably. Wealth is far from evenly distributed both aspatially, within the population, and geographically, from place to place. For example, 16 per cent of American families in 1979 enjoyed an income in excess of $35,000, while 21 per cent received less than $10,000. Indeed, 9 per cent of families lived below the official poverty line. Inter-regional contrasts are also pronounced as the differences in the median incomes of four-person families in 1979 between Alaska ($31,000) and Mississippi ($9999) shows. These differences of wealth are paralleled by pronounced disparities in more general levels of social well-being across the nation. Some inter-personal and inter-regional variation in affluence and quality of life is to be expected in such a large country, but when aggregate wealth and productive capacity are so enormous, the extremely low living standards of those in poverty and in backward areas are matters of legitimate concern. This is especially the case in view of the higher level of social consciousness and responsibility that might be expected in one of the world's most advanced nations. If the production of wealth was the major problem facing industrial America, then its equitable distribution is a central issue facing post-industrial America.

A wide range of policies has been developed over the post-war period to try to reduce the differences of income, opportunity, and social well-being that exist within the United States. This has been a growing concern of government which, as was seen in Chapter 1, has adopted an increasingly interventionist stance over the past forty years with respect to welfare issues. Assistance is made available both directly to individuals via fiscal and welfare schemes, and indirectly by providing aid to the depressed regions in which many of them live. As the measures which are directed specifically at urban residents and areas have been discussed previously, the focus in this chapter is upon distributional imbalances and correctives at a wider spatial scale. Specifically, it examines the dimensions of regional disparity and policies in post-industrial America.

Affluence and poverty

A substantial and continuing rise in the prosperity of the average American ranks as one of the main achievements of the post-war economy. Despite the addition of 75 million to the population between 1950 and 1980, gross national product increased threefold enabling median family incomes to double over the period. Associated with this overall improvement was an extension of wealth to many families that previously subsisted on low incomes. Particularly noticeable is the increase in the number of families in high income brackets, which means that a sizable section of the population is now far removed from the hardship and poverty suffered by their parents and grandparents (Table 6.1). Similarly, the number of families in the lowest income category fell substantially. Despite these changes, the distribution of affluence remains highly skewed. The top 1 per cent of the population own around 20 per cent of personal wealth, a pattern which has changed little over the past half century. The general increase in real incomes has had important implications for individuals' and households' expenditure patterns. The most basic item of expenditure is food, but as incomes rise so more resources can be devoted to housing. As this is a store of value as well as a means of shelter, this affects the rate of equity accumulation and so reinforces wealth differentials. In 1979, 69 per cent of housing was owner-occupied by people who were able to invest in their home and build up equity capital in it. This represents an increase of 10 per cent on the 1955 figure. Most of the remaining occupants in 1979 were tenants, paying rent and acquiring no wealth as a result. Moreover, as the quality of such accommodation is generally lower, renters suffered a further disadvantage. Further indications of the general increase in affluence are shown by the increase in the number of houses with major household appliances. In 1979, 43 per cent of homes had dish-

Table 6.1 *Income characteristics of families, 1955–79*

	Monthly income of families, constant (1979) dollars		Families below poverty line	
	Above 35,000	*Below 10,000*	*Number*	
	%	%	*(000s)*	%
1955	3.1	38.9	N/A	N/A
1960	6.2	32.4	8243	18.1
1965	10.5	26.8	5784	11.8
1970	10.6	21.3	5260	10.1
1975	11.1	22.3	5450	9.7
1979	15.5	20.6	5320	9.1

Source: Statistical Abstract of the United States 1981, Tables 725 and 752.

washers, 45 per cent freezers, 77 per cent washers, and 90 per cent color televisions. Penetration rates for these items in 1960 were 7 per cent, 23 per cent, 55 per cent, and 5 per cent respectively.

Despite the general improvement in living standards, concern must be expressed about the circumstances of those whose incomes are lowest. By no means all Americans have benefited from rising post-war prosperity, indeed very nearly 10 per cent of all families live below the official poverty line (Table 6.1). The concept of poverty is and always has been relative as no single standard is applicable at all times and in all places. The basic difficulty is to decide what level of material deprivation places a family in poverty and then to arrive at an operational definition that can be used for diagnostic purposes. The view of the Social Security Administration in 1964, endorsed by the Federal Interagency Committee in 1969, was that hardship was encountered when a family is forced to spend over one-third of its income on food, as in these circumstances it cannot afford to be both adequately housed and adequately fed. Incorporating adjustments to allow for family size, age, sex, and place of residence, this yardstick provides the basis for the index used by the government in the official definition of poverty. Although the indicator shows that there has been a significant fall in the percentage of poor families over the past thirty years, there has been relatively little change since 1965. Indeed the total number of poor families is substantially the same. Twenty-five million Americans currently subsist below the poverty level, a situation described by Morrill and Wohlenberg (1971, p.2) as an "inexcusable disgrace." It gives rise to fears that the post-industrial economy may be polarizing American society by continually enhancing the position of the wealthy while doing little or nothing to alleviate the conditions of those who are least well-off.

As a group within the population, the poor are not easy to identify. No single reason for poverty exists, although those in particular social and economic categories are particularly susceptible (Table 6.2). Race and ethnic background are especially important considerations as the percentage of poor Blacks is three times, and of those of Spanish origin is twice, that of poor Whites. Similarly, poverty is more prevalent among large families and where the household head is young, a single female, or has a low level of educational attainment. It also tends to arise in families where the householder does not work, whether on accont of unemployment,

Table 6.2   *Families below poverty level: selected characteristics, 1979*

Characteristic	% below poverty level
Total, all races	9.1
White	6.8
Black	27.6
Spanish origin	19.7
Household head	
Age 15 to 24 years	18.7
Less than 8 years elementary education	23.0
Female, no husband present	48.4
Not working	50.8
Size of family	
7 persons or more	24.2
Location	
In central cities	12.7
Outside metropolitan areas	10.8

Source: Statistical Abstract of the United States 1981, Tables 753 and 754.

incapacity, or non-availability. None of these categories, however, is independent and in many cases poverty arises because families are disadvantaged in a number of ways. Indeed the factors involved tend to be reinforcing and self-perpetuating, trapping low-income families into a cycle of poverty from which there is no easy means of escape.

As well as being more common among families in particular socio-economic categories, the incidence of poverty varies markedly from place to place. That there is some concentration of poverty at the local scale is indicated by Table 6.2 which shows that the percentage of poor families in both central cities and non-metropolitan areas is slightly above the national average. However, adjusting income for a variety of deductions and the value of in-kind food and medical care transfers, Seninger and Smeeding (1981, p.383) found that non-metropolitan poverty was more serious than central-city poverty. Rural people benefit to a lesser extent than central-city residents from welfare benefits and services, partly because those services are less accessible in remoter areas. More marked differences of incidence are encountered across the nation with the percentage of families in poverty varying from 20 per cent in Mississippi to a little over 5 per cent in Alaska, Connecticut, Iowa, and Wisconsin. In 1975 the states with the greatest proportion of poor families formed a contiguous grouping in the South and along the Mexican border where, as well as Mississippi, levels of poverty in excess of one-and-a-half times the national average were recorded in Georgia, Louisiana, Arkansas, and New Mexico (Figure 6.1). Analysis at state level, however, necessarily conceals more subtle variations of incidence but these have been examined by Morrill and Wohlenberg (1971) at the level of the state economic area. Although the data are now more than a decade old, their analysis suggests that the geographical incidence of poverty is significantly more extensive than that portrayed in Figure 6.1. They identified a contiguous region of poverty covering the whole of the South from the lower Rio Grande Valley to Alabama whence it divided into two prongs which continued either side of the Appalachian Piedmont through Kentucky on the west, and through North Carolina on the Atlantic coastal plain. Other areas of concentration exist in northern New England and in the northern High Plains. The poorest areas in the South were found to be either lowland farming areas including the Mississippi Delta, the coastal plain, and the tributary areas, with high proportions of Blacks, or the remote and isolated parts of the Ozark–Appalachian uplands. A striking feature of the southern pattern, however, is the relatively greater prosperity of the state economic areas adjacent to the coast and in the industrial Piedmont. For Morrill and Wohlenberg (p.28), these stand out as "islands of affluence in a sea of poverty."

The characteristics of poverty in the South were illustrated in 1970 by the United States Department of Agriculture's report on *Rural Poverty in Three Southern States*. Two of the areas analyzed in particular detail were the Mississippi Delta and South Carolina, the latter being considered representative of the southern coastal plain. About half of the families interviewed in these two areas were Black but around 80 per cent of Blacks were found to be poor. In these two areas, Blacks are landless and although traditionally working as farm laborers and sharecroppers, the increasing scale and mechanization of farming, as discussed in Chapter 5, have reduced local employment opportunities. While educational levels are strongly correlated with poverty status among Whites, they are less important among Blacks. The authors of the report found that when the various factors generally associated with poverty, such as

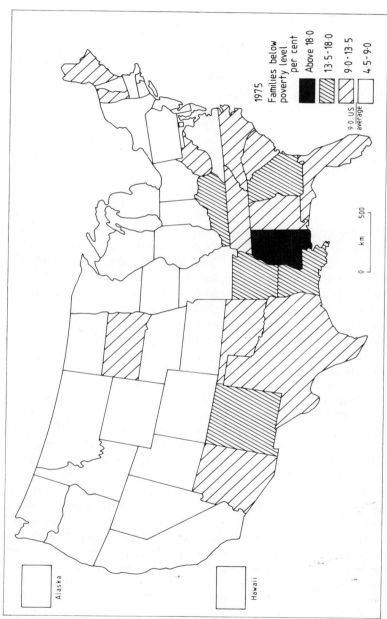

Figure 6.1 *The percentage of families below the poverty level, 1975*

age, occupation, and household size, were cross classified by race, many of the relationships between these factors and poverty were reduced in the strength of their association. Although these socio-economic characteristics are not unimportant, race was the overriding influence affecting poverty in the area.

Although poor Blacks are more numerous, the poor Whites in the South, and in the Piedmont and plateaux of the Appalachians and Ozarks have been disadvantaged for longer. They date back to the indentured laborers brought over from England for the initial development of the region. Watson (1979) explains that when their period of service ended, they left the towns and plantations and settled in the "back country" areas, which, because of the spread of settlement, became increasingly remote and isolated. Equally, these were the areas of most marginal agricultural land. For Watson, their ruling passion was to remain free, so they found it difficult to participate in Southern society. In consequence, many were illiterate, unable to count, never took part in public affairs, and paid no taxes, all of which further increased their social isolation. "It is not true to say that many southern whites were poor because of their rugged and difficult environment. Rather, they sought that environment out because of the social values that made them poor" (p. 131). The incidence of poverty in large parts of the South is accentuated by the severe and persistent social and economic problems of Appalachia. As a physical region, Appalachia cuts diagonally through thirteen states from southern New York to northern Mississippi and includes the whole of West Virginia, most of Pennsylvania, but only a very small corner of Maryland and South Carolina (Figure 6.2). Appalachia is home for 20 million people or one out of eleven Americans. Poverty levels vary widely within the region but, with the exception of New York and Pennsylvania, are well above the national figure (Table 6.3). In consequence, Appalachia comprises the most extensive area of concentrated poverty in the nation.

The problems of Appalachia are a complex product of geographical, historical, economic, and social factors. In physical terms, the area consists of the Appalachian Plateau, the Ridge and Valley province, the Blue Ridge, and the Piedmont Plateau which together, because of their longitudinal alignment, form a serious barrier to east-west movement. In particular, at the heart of the system, the Blue Ridge and Ridge and Valley province divide the landscape into a corrugation of depressions and forested hills

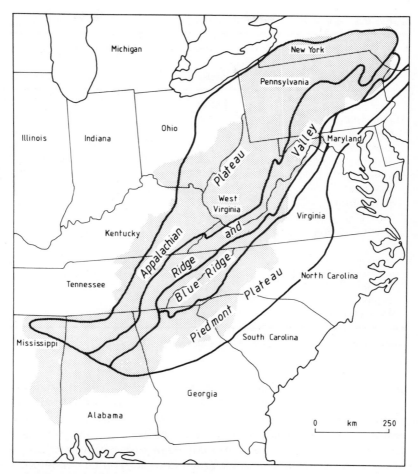

Figure 6.2 *Appalachia*

which can neither be crossed easily nor readily cultivated. Moreover, they constrain the size of hinterlands, thereby inhibiting the
growth of towns so that the area remains predominantly rural in
character. As a consequence of folding and faulting, many coal and
mineral deposits lie close to the surface so the area has been heavily
exploited for its mineral wealth. Indeed, ease of extraction enabled
open-cast methods, which despoiled the landscape on an extensive

Table 6.3 *Appalachia: levels of poverty, 1975*

	Persons below poverty level, 1975	
	(000s)	*% of 1975 population*
United States	24,934	11.8
Appalachian region	2774	15.0
Appalachian portion of:		
Alabama	367	16.5
Georgia	148	15.0
Kentucky	279	29.0
Maryland	27	13.0
Mississippi	113	25.5
New York	101	9.5
North Carolina	177	16.0
Ohio	157	13.5
Pennsylvania	605	10.0
South Carolina	90	12.5
Tennessee	336	18.0
Virginia	90	18.0
West Virginia	298	16.0

Source: Statistical Abstract of the United States 1981, Table 758.

scale, to be used in many areas. Appalachia remained relatively prosperous as long as the demand for coal was buoyant, but when markets began to contract, the extent of the narrowness of the region's economic base became apparent. First in the depression years of the 1930s and then in the course of post-war rationalization of industry, unemployment became endemic. The lack of alternative jobs presented out-of-work miners with two choices: either to live on welfare, or to leave the area altogether.

Against this general background, the more detailed reasons for poverty in Appalachia were analyzed in the 1964 Report of the President's Appalachian Regional Commission (PARC, 1964). Although the physical difficulties and limitations of Appalachia were recognized, the report underlined the resources and developmental potential of Appalachia and attributed its economic problems to poor exploitive practices and the failure of the mine and resource owners to re-invest some of the substantial wealth in the region. Thus in changing national circumstances, including the decline of coal and changes in farming practices, the region was left behind in terms of economic growth, with dire results. Between 1950 and 1960, the report noted, employment in the United States outside Appalachia expanded by 17 per cent, while in Appalachia it fell by 1.5 per cent. Unemployment was thus far ahead of the national average and with low levels of labor force participation, the "effective" unemployment rate was 15 per cent for males and 21 per cent for females. Even when in employment, Appalachian workers often earned wages insufficient to maintain their families above the poverty line. The report thus estimated that in addition to the 1.1 million effectively unemployed there were a further three-quarters of a million "working poor." Numerous difficulties flowed from these conditions including very poor quality of housing, low levels of retail sales and savings, inadequate health and educational services, and a heavy dependence upon public assistance.

The scale of the problem would have been greater without a net migration of 2 million people from the region between 1950 and 1960. In consequence, and despite the fact that the birth rate remained at or above the national average, the population of Appalachia grew by a mere 1 per cent over the decade. Out-migration, moreover, altered the age structure of the population resulting in a major rise in the numbers aged over 65. Although these demographic trends had some effects on the distribution of population, the growth of urban centers was comparatively sluggish. Such urban centers as existed in the area were predominantly small and there was a notable lack of larger metropolitan places of the kind that, at that time, were the focus of economic and social advance. Some important changes have taken place in Appalachia in the twenty years since the report was published, but its analysis of the origins of poverty remains relevant today. No single cause can be held to be responsible; rather its origins lie in the complex of geographical, historical, social, and economic circumstances which disadvantage both the area in general and the people who live in it.

Similar considerations explain and account for the incidence of poverty in the South-West. Here, low income families are predominantly Native American (Indian), or of Spanish origin, and poverty is a product of the complex historical and cultural factors which maintain the social and geographical isolation of ethnic and racial groups. In 1980, those of Spanish origin in the United States numbered some 14.6 million, and included the Hispanos of New Mexico (who have resided in that area since the seventeenth century); Mexican American Chicanos, both legal immigrants and their descendants as well as aliens; Cuban Americans, and recent Cuban emigrees; Puerto Ricans resident in the United States; and immigrant and alien Latin Americans. Some 5.5 million of them, notably Hispanos and Chicanos, lived in the states of California, Arizona, and New Mexico. The work of Meyer (1983) suggests that the South-West is the area of most concentrated poverty for the Spanish heritage people. In the mid-seventies, 23 per cent of the Mexican-origin families in the area lived below the poverty level. The reasons for their low incomes are complex and stem from their cultural isolation and separateness, which is manifest in terms of low levels of formal education and training, language problems which inhibit assimilation, the concentration of employment in blue-collar jobs, and discrimination (Tienda, 1981). A complicating factor in the Spanish-heritage population's relation to the majority society is the continual flow of legal and illegal migrants into the area which adds to the pool of unskilled and inexperienced labor (McPheters and Schlagenhauf, 1981). Early marriage and large families are characteristic traits of Spanish-heritage groups, both of which tend to produce unfavorable dependency ratios within the family unit.

At first glance, poverty among Native Americans (Indians) may be linked to lack of economic opportunity since most Native Americans (Indians) in the South-West live on reservations in California, Oklahoma, New Mexico, and Arizona, where the number and range of jobs are limited (Table 6.4). Moreover, the level of participation in the labor force of those Native Americans (Indians) who live on reservations tends to be low as Vinje (1977) has shown. Poverty among non-reservation Native Americans (Indians) in urban areas where there are many more openings is, however, equally severe and this suggests that the origins of the problem may lie in the inability or unwillingness of Native Americans (Indians) to compete within the job market. Economic disadvantage tends to be compounded by social circumstances relating to large family size and the large number of young children. Together these factors suggest that poverty among Native Americans (Indians) is strongly related to their alienation from, and low level of participation in, mainstream social and economic life.

Table 6.4 *The distribution of Native Americans*[1]

	Number (000s)	% of state population
United States	1418.0	–
California	201.3	0.9
Oklahoma	169.5	5.6
Arizona	152.9	5.6
New Mexico	104.8	8.1
North Carolina	64.6	1.1
Alaska	64.0	16.0
Washington	60.8	1.5
South Dakota	45.1	6.5
Michigan	40.0	0.4

Note: [1]Includes Indians, Eskimos and Aleutians.
Source: Statistical Abstracts of the United States 1981, Table 36.

The social and spatial segregation of Native Americans (Indians) reflects the wide gap which separates the indigenous and White populations and cultures in contemporary America. Although the "melting pot" effect has, over the years, blurred many ethnic and racial distinctions, Native Americans (Indians) remain largely unassimilated. One reason is the sheer size of the cultural distance between primitive hunting/gathering systems and societies, and mainstream post-industrialism. Many Native Americans (Indians) are unable to adjust their tribal values to accommodate the needs of the time-regulated, credit-card based, media-intensive, high technology service economy (Durant and Knowlton, 1978; Murray and Tweeten, 1981). The other is that Native Americans (Indians) in recent years have made conscious attempts to resist integration and to re-assert their right to an independent existence and self-determination. Violent incidents such as the occupation of Alcatraz jail in 1969–71, the invasion of the Bureau of Indian Affairs in Washington in 1972, and the symbolic and bitter stand at Wounded Knee, South Dakota, in 1973, drew attention to their separate identity. At the same time, demands were made for a re-negotiation of Indian treaties, and the return of lands lost since the original agreements were made between the Native Americans (Indians) and the United States. They also wished to democratize tribal government, to receive federal aid directly instead of through federal officials, and for Native Americans (Indians) in cities to be provided with proper training, work, and housing programs. Whatever the justification for these demands, their effect is to further increase the isolation of Indian groups.

Native Americans (Indians) comprise a small but exceptionally needy minority group. They are not only poor in material goods, but are widely impoverished in spirit. This is due to a long period of dependence upon society at large, as well as concern and apprehension about the future. More than a century of social isolation in separate enclaves has taken its toll on initiative, creativity, and independent thought and action. Although the size of the Native American (Indian) population is not known, estimates range from 0.9 to 1.4 million. Even accepting the latter figure, the Native American (Indian) population represents a relatively small proportion of the total poor. The task of ameliorating their poverty should not be an unsuperable undertaking for a country as affluent and tolerant as the United States.

Social well-being

Variations among the population in levels of income form an important strand in a more general pattern of areal differences in welfare within the United States. Regional gradients in levels of living are not as pronounced as they were at mid-century but significant differentials remain. These mean that people residing in some states enjoy a markedly better quality of life and prospects than those living elsewhere. As well as incomes, such differences include physical health and state-of-mind, three dimensions which for Smith (1973) define the level of social well-being. As a concept, social well-being is essentially multivariate and involves a consideration of the major personal, social, economic, and environmental factors which determine the quality of life in a particular area. Levels of social well-being provide an important measure of the social state of the nation.

In analyzing levels of social well-being in 1973, Smith considered forty-seven territorial social indicators. Eleven measures were concerned with income and wealth, employment status and welfare benefits. They were chosen so as to reflect not only the availability of money to provide access to the goods and services that fulfilled needs and bring satisfaction, but also the importance of employment and the capacity for self-support as measures of personal status in a society that places high value on economic achievement. Environmental quality was indicated by three housing variables, while health, subdivided into three categories of physical health, access to medical care, and mental health, was considered by means of ten measures. Six educational parameters concerned with achievement, duration in full-time education, and levels of provision comprised the next sub-group, while the remaining variables were concerned with social disorganization and alienation/participation. The former set consisted of ten indicators which measured personal pathologies such as disease, alcohol and drug addiction, family breakdown, and crime and safety. The latter indexed levels of political involvement, criminality, and social segregation. Not all the variables were equal in importance and several were surrogates rather than direct indicators. But together they provided a comprehensive and wide-ranging measure of the social health of each state.

By combining standard scores of the variables in each group, and mapping the results, Smith identified spatial variations in the major dimensions of social well-being (Figure 6.3). The most important finding was that with the exception of social disorganization, the same pattern of inter-regional variation in social well-being was identified by all the measures. In each case, the lowest scoring states comprise a highly concentrated cluster in the South. In fact, Alabama, Arkansas, Georgia, Louisiana, Mississippi, and the Carolinas all fall into the bottom twelve states on each of the five criteria. The top twelve states show a little more variation although Connecticut and Massachusetts appear in all five, and Utah, Washington, and Wisconsin in four of the five. In the social disorganization map, the concentration of bottom states shifts to the north-western corner of the nation and includes none of the eight southern states which appear on all the other maps. More detailed analysis led Smith to argue that this pattern was strongly related to the level of population stability as the incidence of pathologies such as high crime, alcoholism, and venereal disease is high in states with the worst scores on the social disorganization indicator. The most important conclusion, however, is that despite its post-war revival, levels of social well-being, whether measured in

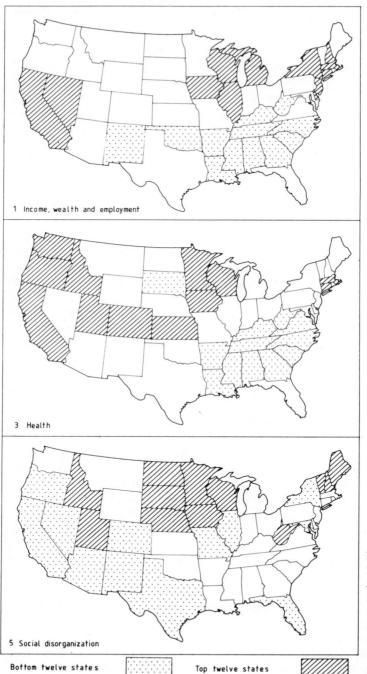

1 Income, wealth and employment

3 Health

5 Social disorganization

Bottom twelve states · · · · · · · · · Top twelve states ///////

Figure 6.3
The geography of social well-being Source: *Smith (1973, p. 88). Reproduced with kind permission of McGraw-Hill Book Company.*

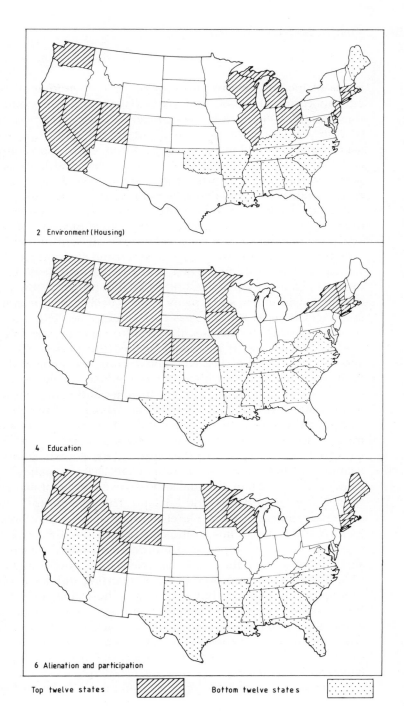

2 Environment (Housing)

4 Education

6 Alienation and participation

Figure 6.3
Continued

Top twelve states ▨ Bottom twelve states ⠿

terms of income, wealth and employment, environment, health, education, or alienation and participation are consistently low throughout the South. Moreover, social well-being improves steadily with increasing distance away from the South, the highest scoring states overall being New York, Connecticut, Massachusetts, and California. The comparative economic backwardness of large parts of the South is well documented, but Smith's analysis demonstrates that it is a socially depressed area as well.

Of all the social indicators used in Smith's analysis, the incidence of crime is perhaps the most powerful single measure of general social well-being, since it reflects both the amount of deprivation and disadvantage and the degree of strain and stress in society. For Johnston (1982) two types of crime can be identified. The first involves economic crimes or crimes against property, the majority of which involve theft and larceny. Poverty itself is likely to stimulate such activity as is the idleness that comes with long periods of unemployment. The stresses that result in mental instability can lead to the second type, crimes against the person. Child and spouse battering are very common among the poor and many homicides take place within the immediate family as indirect consequences of both living on low incomes and in depressing and inadequate environments. Despite the passage of two hundred years since Crevècoeur (1782) identified the "love of violence" as intrinsic to the American character, levels of serious crime remain far in excess of those in other leading developed nations. For example in 1978, the homicide rate per 100,000 population was 9.4 as compared to 2.6 in Canada, and below 2.0 in Australia, France, Norway, the Netherlands, and England. The most recent statistics, moreover, indicate that the level of criminality is increasing. The incidence of violent crime, as indicated by the number of robberies, aggravated assaults, rapes, and murders and non-negligent manslaughters known to the police, has risen sharply over the post-war period (Figure 6.4). Improved levels of reporting and detection may be contributory factors but the trends show that an extremely violent society is becoming progressively more violent. If the level of crime is some reflection of personal satisfaction with lifestyle and environment, then the post-industrial economy, which has done so much to raise average levels of income, has been a comparative failure in social terms.

Crime, especially violent crime, is an emotive social issue because

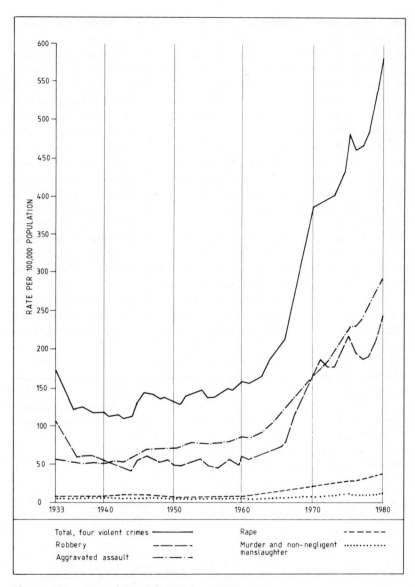

Figure 6.4 *Trends in violent crime, 1950–80*

it is prevalent in particular localities. Significant regional variations in criminality exist, but these are far less important than those which separate rural and urban areas. The metropolitan areas have the worst incidence as the rate of violent crime in major cities is up to four times the national average (Table 6.5). Furthermore, it is higher the larger the city. Violence in the city arises because urban life both adds to the tensions and deepens the divisions out of which conflict springs, as well as supplying the anonymity and fluidity that assists the criminal. Moreover, cities are where economic values dominate and give rise to the fiercest competition and strongest emphasis upon success. A further factor may be that the design of urban environments is more conducive to crime. Public areas such as parking lots, corridors, stairways, and elevators are not part of any individual's or household's territory and, as no-man's lands, are spaces in which residents can be harassed or attacked. The rising level of crime in major cities is a deeply disturbing trend and is a factor in the increasing out-migration of mobile middle classes in recent years.

Variations in levels of affluence and social well-being within the population and from place to place are the product of complex causes. People may be socially deprived because they are members

Table 6.5   *Crime rates for violent crimes[1], 1980*

Location	Number known to police per 100,000 population
United States	581
Cities with populations of 250,000 or more	1414
Cities with populations 10,000 to 25,000	352
Selected cities	
New York	2126
Baltimore	2112
Washington	2011
Detroit	1945
San Francisco	1885
Los Angeles	1742

Note: [1]Offences of murder and non-negligent manslaughter, rape, robbery, and aggravated assault.

Source: Statistical Abstract of the United States 1981, Table 296.

of disadvantaged racial, ethnic, educational, and income groups, or because they live in parts of the country where there are few jobs, predominantly low paid jobs, or poor social facilities and opportunities. Aspatial and geographical causes of deprivation are frequently self-reinforcing but tend to be tackled by different means. Thus the fiscal and welfare schemes outlined in the preceding chapter, which apply to people wherever they live, are paralleled by provision of aid and assistance to particular localities. These seek to promote underlying social and economic change and so assist individuals and families indirectly and on a permanent basis. That regional differentials are persistent has given rise to important changes in the character of regional planning and policy over the post-war period.

Area development planning and policy

Although severe regional disparities have persisted in the United States throughout the post-war period, area development planning is very much a feature of the last twenty years. In the immediate post-war period, rising affluence and the increasing level of national awareness made possible by the plane, the telephone, and television, brought into sharp focus those regions which were failing to share in the general prosperity of the nation. Federal intervention was considered, but as this raised issues of principle concerning the role that the government should play in the economic life of the nation, action was not forthcoming. After 1955, the unacceptable nature of the disparities led Senator Douglas of Illinois to lobby vigorously for legislation to deal with regional economic distress, but it took a rise in unemployment in the run-up to the 1960 presidential elections to make aid to depressed areas a political issue. National television coverage of the West Virginia primary, in particular, drew public attention to the serious problems of the state and of Appalachia, and Senator Kennedy made aid to depressed areas a major plank in his platform. Priority action was promised if he was elected. As a consequence, the Area Redevelopment Act, the first major piece of legislation of the Kennedy Administration, was passed in 1961.

The basic idea of the ARA program was to make economic

development assistance available to any eligible region. These were those which had persistent unemployment that exceeded the national average by a stated amount, or which had median incomes a stated percentage lower than the national median. The aid was in the form of technical assistance in planning, loans and grants for the construction of public facilities, and low interest loans to private business firms. As such it was deliberately discriminatory, helping some pre-determined areas and not others. Within these areas, it was assumed that aid would somehow reach needy families and individuals (Cumberland, 1971). Inevitably, the definition of regions eligible for aid became a critical issue for the Area Development Administration, especially as speedy action, which of necessity precluded much background research, was expected. The basic units used were the Bureau of Employment Security Areas which usually had a labor force of at least 15,000, including 8000 in non-agricultural employment. The criteria for inclusion was the numbers out of work. A large number of counties containing small urban areas were also added on the basis of income levels, as were counties selected by the Department of Agriculture under its rural development program. Finally, Indian reservations were defined as economic areas eligible for aid. The result was that by 1963, over 1000 areas were designated with a least one in every state (Figure 6.5). These ranged from extreme rural areas with sparse population but few employment opportunities, to large urban areas like Pittsburgh and Detroit where there were chronic labor surpluses.

The assistance offered to designated areas under the ARA program was of four major types. These were: loans to businesses, loans and grants for constructing public facilities, measures to retrain the unemployed, and research and technical assistance. To qualify for aid, each Redevelopment Area had to elect a committee representative of important local interests to produce on Overall Economic Development Program (OEDP) which analyzed the problems of the area and presented the case for stimulating local economic growth. Loans to businesses were intended to assist in construction rather than with capital accumulation or relocation expenses. Assurances had to be given that more than temporary employment would be created, and that finance was not otherwise available. Moreover, 10 per cent of the total sums required had to come from local sources. Similar arrangements applied to loans for public buildings but with the provisos that the community should

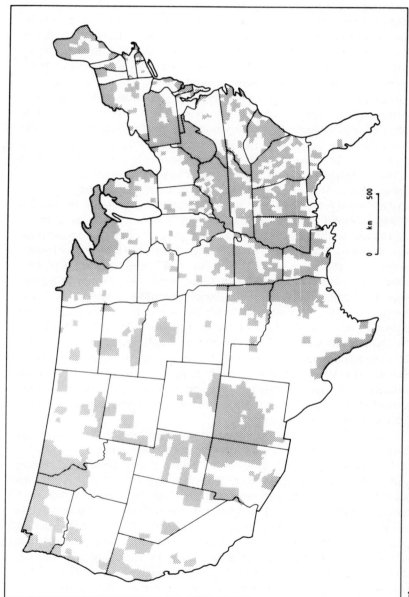

Figure 6.5   *Assisted areas as defined by the Area Redevelopment Administration, 1963.*

contribute to the cost according to its ability, and that the project could not otherwise be undertaken. Most funding was provided for tourist and recreational projects, which have a particularly favorable cost per job ratio, and for the construction of industrial parks and utilities (Levitan, 1964). Far smaller amounts were allocated for technical assistance and labor retraining.

In establishing the legitimacy of comprehensive regional aid and demonstrating that channeling public funds into regions of low incomes and chronic unemployment was both socially acceptable and politically beneficial, the ARA was a significant success. In a more practical sense, however, its achievements were more limited as the number of direct jobs created was estimated in the final report of the ARA at only 71,400 (Estall, 1972). Assuming a ratio of two indirect jobs for every three direct, ARA projects helped to provide about 118,000 new jobs between 1961 and 1965. As national unemployment fell by 1.3 million over the period, this contribution was minimal. For Levitan (1964), important shortcomings characterized the ARA program. The first was the undue emphasis placed upon physical development, largely because construction interests were in a majority on many local area committees. The second was the poor quality of many OEDP plans, as a consequence of lack of expertise, resources, and leadership at the local level. The third was the inadequate size and lack of functional coherence of many of the development regions. These deficiencies at a local level were paralleled in Washington by administrative shortcomings caused by limitations of staff and budget. For these reasons, the program was re-cast and expanded in 1965 by the Public Works and Economic Development Act.

In place of the ARA, the Act created the Economic Development Administration. Its task was to correct the deficiencies of the ARA but without innovating to such an extent that it generated public and congressional opposition (Cumberland, 1971). Although the basic forms of assistance remained substantially the same, the EDA had a fivefold increase in budget and placed a far greater emphasis upon grants rather than loans expenditure. The most important change was the creation of a new set of planning areas. In addition to the ADA's redevelopment areas, many of which were retained, the Act defined multi-county development districts, each of which contained two or more redevelopment areas and at least one development center. These formed the chief area planning unit. At a much wider scale, provision was made for two or more contiguous states that were related geographically and culturally, and which lagged behind the nation in economic development and rates of growth, to join together and request the designation of an Economic Development Region to cover appropriate areas of the states. On designation, a joint federal-state commission would be established to prepare long-range economic development plans to guide federal, state and other development agencies in drawing up action programs. By 1967, five Economic Development Regions had been created covering twenty states in whole or in part, with a population of some 25 million (Figure 6.6).

The regions designated varied widely in terms of their social and economic problems, and hence the ameliorative policies that were required. New England was most distinctive because it was an advanced urban–industrial area suffering long-term decline on account of de-industrialization and out-migration. Particularly serious was the unemployment in southern New England cities caused by the contraction of the traditional textile, shoe, and leather industries, which, combined with the outdated infrastructure of these centers, made them unattractive to investment. At the same time, there was widespread rural poverty in northern New England on account of its distance and remoteness from the major growth centers in the nation. Many similarities exist between this area and the four other regions which are consistently poor and rural in character. The Upper Great Lakes is a region of some former prosperity based upon its mineral wealth, but it was suffering from isolation and the lack of urban centers large enough to attract new economic activities into the area. For this reason, Berry's (1973a) plan, based upon a comprehensive analysis of the problems and needs of the region, envisaged identifying and then concentrating public investment and planning efforts into potential growth centers. The Four Corners Region comprised 8 per cent of the total United States land mass including a vast tract of territory that was federally owned. It contained large Indian reservations and the overriding issue for the Commission was to design constructive programs to meet the needs of the Indians without destroying their cultural heritage, values, and environment. Important racial and ethnic dimensions also compounded the problems of limited economic opportunity and poverty that existed in the Ozarks and Coastal Plains. All five regions suffered from geographical remote-

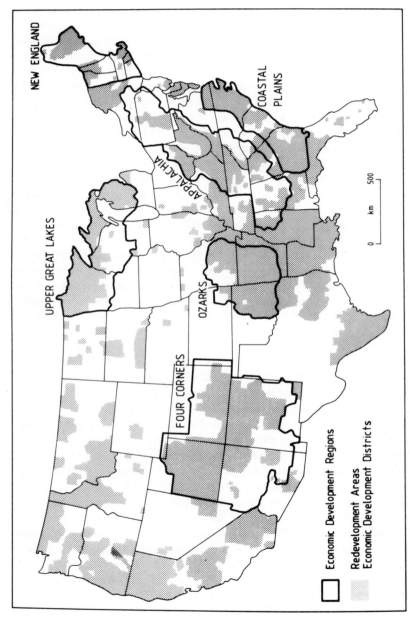

Figure 6.6 *Economic Development Regions, 1967*

ness and isolation, which in turn contributed to their economic and social backwardness.

The Appalachian Economic Development Region which is shown is Figure 6.6 was also designated in 1965 but under the Appalachian Regional Development Act. This followed from the report of the President's Appalachian Regional Commission which argued that Appalachia should be treated as one unit as the problem was "first and last a regional one which will yield only to regionwide attack as hard in concept as it is in geographical area" (PARC, 1964). Although the Economic Development Regions were similar in geographical terms, the Appalachian Regional Commission, because of its separate background and designation, differed from the other Regional Planning Commissions in administrative and financial terms, as Estall (1982) emphasized. In common with the other Economic Redevelopment Commissions, the Appalachian Regional Commission is a comprehensive planning agency with federal authority to produce a multi-state plan, but it is controlled not by federal or state governments acting separately, but by a membership comprising both state and federal representatives. The Commission thus "straddles both tiers of government and is in a sense independent of both in framing proposals and recommendations" (Estall 1982, p.38). A second difference is that the multi-county development districts through which county and city authorities are represented have a mandatory role in planning. A third is that the Appalachian Regional Commission is more than a planning agency as it has sizeable funds with which to implement its plans in terms of development projects. These differences mean that the achievements of the Appalachian Regional Commission must be assessed separately from those of the other five Economic Development Regions.

In his highly detailed analysis of recent developments in United States regional planning, Estall (1982) maintains that, with the exception of Appalachia, the Economic Development Regions "have largely failed in their task of promoting the economic development of lagging regions" (p. 37). Little evidence is available to suggest that unemployment has been reduced, and poverty in parts of the region remains well in excess of the national average. Indeed, the Commissions "have been virtually invisible, their existence possibly unsuspected by the majority of the populations for whose futures they were created to plan" (p. 35). Numerous reasons account for these shortcomings, the most important being the very low level of funding (Estall, 1977). Between 1965 and 1975, only about $260 million was made available for the Commissions' work, an insignificant amount compared with the scale of the needs of the regions concerned. Moreover, it was only a tiny fraction of the total sums, themselves quite small in amount, appropriated over the decade for other purposes of the 1965 regional development program. The low level of support reflected "the indifference or even hostility of successive federal Administrations and a generally unproductive relationship with the EDA" (p. 35). Moreover, it meant that the Commissions were restricted to a planning rather than an implementation role. With Congress support, the five Commissions continued in existence but, with inadequate funding, they achieved little.

In contrast to the poor performance of the other five industrial development regions, circumstances in Appalachia improved significantly. Between 1965 and 1980, numerous new jobs were created in the area, per capita incomes rose progressively, and both unemployment and poverty levels fell more into line with national averages. Total population grew by about 1.1 million between 1970 and 1977, more than double the increase of the entire 1960–70 decade. Moreover a rise in the size of the in-migrational component attested to the increased attractiveness of the area. Important variations in the levels of prosperity still exist within the region, but the positive recent performance contrasts sharply with the stagnation and decline of the preceding half century (House, 1983).

For Estall (1982), the revival of Appalachia is primarily a product of more favorable national employment and demographic trends. Appalachia has always been an energy-rich region and, while it suffered as a result of the swing towards oil, it has benefited from the recent rise in the demand for coal. A second reason for growth has been the reversal in the long-established pattern of rural–urban migration, associated with the expansion of non-metropolitan areas, which has revived numerous small centers in the region. A third factor is the regional shift in the balance of development from North to South which has enhanced a large part of southern Appalachia in industrial and general economic growth (Estall, 1980).

Against the background of these favorable trends, Estall (1982) argues that the Appalachian Regional Commission has played a beneficial role in assisting economic change in the region. Its most important contribution was in improving key features of the infra-structure including roads, water supplies, sewerage systems, and industrial sites, which enhanced the development potential of the area, and enabled industry, once established, to prosper. Foremost among the initiatives was that of road construction, for some two-thirds of the Commission's budget between 1965 and 1980 was spent on highways. Although the national interstate highway system traversed the region, one of the major conclusions of the President's Appalachian Regional Commission Report (1964) was that remoteness and isolation were major reasons for economic backwardness. In accepting this argument, the Appalachian Regional Commission, after 1965, undertook to plan and build over 3000 miles of "development highway" and "local access road" to connect all parts of the area to the interstate network, some 1700 miles of which were either completed or were under construction by 1978. Several critics questioned the value of highway construction in Appalachia, arguing that it was ill-conceived (Gauthier, 1973), excessively expensive (Munro, 1969) and counter-productive in that it benefited adjacent metropolitan areas, whose hinterlands were effectively extended, rather than Appalachia itself (Hale and Walters, 1974). In response, the Commission justified the highway program on grounds of its practical benefits to industry and employment. Over 60 per cent of new industries (representing 200,000 jobs) attracted to the region between 1970 and 1975 were found to be located within 20 minutes travel time of a new highway (Estall, 1982).

Since 1965, the Appalachian Regional Commission has spent one-third of its budget on non-highway projects. Most of this investment was directed to health, vocational, educational, and community development programs, but environmental improvement and back-ground research work was also supported. Like highway construction, these programs, by improving social conditions, probably helped to encourage industry and population into the area. Estall (1982) concludes that overall, given the size of its budget, the Appalachian Regional Commission has some quite impressive results to show. "Perhaps a balanced judgement of its role to date is that, in the overall context, it has been small but positive, while in particular local circumstances it has been highly significant" (p. 52).

The comparative success of the Appalachian Regional Commission was used as an argument for extensions and additions to the

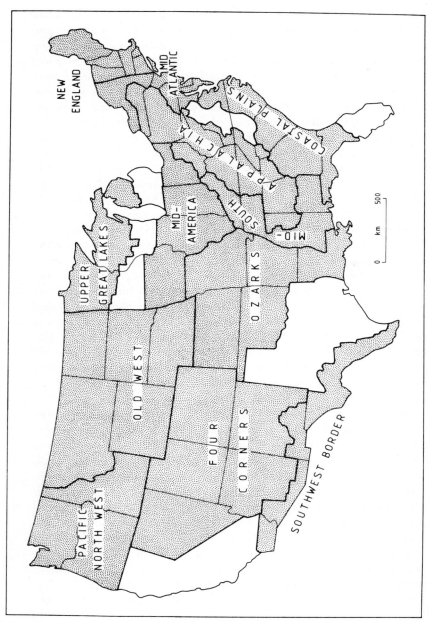

Figure 6.7 *Economic Development Regions, 1980*

other Economic Development Regions. In the early 1970s, two new Commissions were set up and three others substantially expanded (OECD, 1980). The new regions were in the Pacific North-West (the entire states of Washington, Oregon, and Idaho) and the Old West (the entire states of Montana, North and South Dakota, Wyoming, and Nebraska), while the Four Corners, Ozarks, and Coastal Plains Regions were extended. Further changes occurred in the late 1970s with the creation of the Mid-America, Mid-South, and Mid-Atlantic Regions, and South-West Border Regions, so that the system now involves every conterminous state but with parts of eight states excluded (Figure 6.7). A second change was that the historically narrow brief for areas of high unemployment, poverty, and decline was relaxed. Today, the Regional Commissions are broadly involved in the whole process of growth and change, stimulating economic and social developments in some areas, while dealing with problems of over-rapid expansion elsewhere.

Conclusion

America is a rich nation. Average per capita incomes are extremely high, and the population overall is better fed, better housed, and more highly educated than in any other comparable country. The distribution of wealth, however, is far from even both within the population and from place to place. A very small minority of the population own a large share of the nation's personal wealth, while very nearly 10 per cent live below the official poverty line. The number of low income families is similarly high throughout the South, whereas in several Northern and Mid-Western states the incidence of poverty is less than half the national average. Regions of acute poverty exist both because areas of the country are deficient in natural resources and are disadvantaged by remoteness and inaccessibility, and because low income groups tend to be concentrated, through force of economic circumstances, in particular localities. Wealth combines with a range of social, environmental, and economic criteria to define an idea of social well-being which also varies widely across the nation. Minimization of economic differentials was argued as the main justification for regional planning at mid-century, and reliance was placed upon public expenditure and fiscal measures to help backward areas achieve parity with other regions. The need to promote regional balances in economic opportunity remains, but the emergence of a new social consciousness in recent years is seen in the concern for social justice, security, redress of inequalities, and the quality of human life.

The extension in the number and alteration in the role of the Regional Commissions reflects a recognition of how much the geography of the United States has changed over the post-war period. Forty years ago, regional imbalances were primarily a product of rapid population growth, rural to urban, and south to north and west, migration, and of the centralization of economic activity which advanced the fortunes of the manufacturing core at the expense of the resource-rich periphery. In consequence, the North-East and Mid-West were regions of growth and affluence, while stagnation and impoverishment increased with distance away from the center. Today, a different set of processes is creating new spatial patterns and problems. Overall population has stabilized, net rural migration has ended, and deconcentration, both at the local level and across the nation, is taking place. Manufacturing is no longer the source of employment growth, and the emphasis is upon advanced technology and the quaternary and quinary sectors. Acute difficulties, in consequence, are being experienced in the cities, especially in the older industrial regions. Resource-based areas are stronger, and environmental considerations dominate in determining the relative advantages and attractions of different areas. The North-East and Mid-West rather than the South and West have become lagging regions, and the latter are approaching parity. The geography of economic and social health, both locally and at the regional scale, has been inverted, with many areas of mid-century prosperity now experiencing stagnation and decline.

In analyzing the geography of post-industrial America, this book has argued that the formative processes originate in the structure of society and the economy. They are a corollary of the type of social formation, defined by a wide range of social and economic dimensions, that exists at a particular time. Underlying the geography of the United States is a pattern determined by processes distinctive to the high mass-consumption industrial era which prevailed throughout the last twenty-five years of the nineteenth and the first half of the twentieth centuries. The predominant feature of this formation was the central importance of goods production, an emphasis which gave rise to, and in turn was made possible by, a distinctive social and spatial organization. Its elements are seen in the prominence of the business firm; the semi-skilled worker and engineer; property, political organization and technical skill; and inheritance, patronage, and education (Table 1.1). As manufacturing was the leading economic sector, so the spatial structure at mid-century was dictated by the distribution of heavy industry. The economics of least cost and maximum market access location, compounded by the economics of agglomeration and scale, and reinforced by strong forces of inertia, were together responsible for the creation and maintenance of the manufacturing belt, in which production was concentrated in and around a small number of major industrial centers. These acted as poles of change, creating new products and technologies in a cycle of repetitive innovation that maintained the comparative advantages of the heartland over the dependent hinterland. Outside the core area, rates of economic growth and levels of prosperity were restricted by the relative absence of manufacturing. Raw material sources and energy supplies were undervalued as locational assets, and out-migration limited the role played by population increase in market expansion and economic development. Variations within this core-periphery pattern were associated with the distribution of urban centers across the nation which created a distinction between urban and rural America. The geographical pattern at this local scale was similarly urban-centered as the associated processes of rural out-migration and central business district growth underlined. Centrality, agglomeration, distance decay, and physical accessibility, supporting heartlands and hinterlands both locally and across the nation, were the overriding principles which determined the geographical arrangement of industrial America.

This background pattern has been overlain and transformed to a greater or lesser degree since mid-century by population, industrial, agricultural, urban, and regional distributions which serve the needs of the post-industrial society. A deep-seated change in the social formation, involving the rise of the service economy, has taken and is taking place. Its central characteristics are seen in the expansion of quaternary and quinary sector employment, the rise to eminence of professionals, scientists, researchers, and technicians, and the increased importance of information, theoretical knowledge, and scientific decision making (Table 1.1). By far the most important geographical corollary of structural change is the greatly increased degree of locational flexibility which has been made possible. Freedom of choice has replaced locational constraint and universal accessibility has superseded simple distance decay so removing the traditional premium on centrality. Against this background, new and previously unimportant considerations now figure prominently in many locational decisions. Quality of life and quality of environment now at least equal, and in many cases are more important than, least cost and maximum market access as factors in locational choice, as shown by the increased attractiveness of sunbelt states and rural areas. In consequence, non-central areas, both locally and across the nation, are expanding at the expense of the traditional urban and industrial cores. The geography of population and of industry, and of cities and regions, is being transformed, even inverted, as structural changes produce, and are facilitated by, a complex set of radical geographical adjustments.

The superimposition of post-industrial elements upon an underlying industrial pattern means that the geography of contemporary America must be viewed as an amalgam of recent and relic components. To reach this conclusion by taking snapshot views at only two points in time, mid-century and today, is however to ignore the on-going nature of societal evolution and geographical response. It is to imply an element of stillness in what is essentially a continuous and incremental process of change. As an integral part of the social and economic structure, the geographical pattern is in a perpetual state of flux. In succeeding colonialism, frontier agriculturalism, and industrialism, post-industrial society is merely the most recent social formation to impose its distinctive imprint on the geography of the United States of America.

References

Abler, R. (1975) *Human Geography in a Shrinking World*, North Scitaute, Mass.: Duxbury.

Abler, R. and Adams, J.S. (1976) *Comparative Atlas of America's Great Cities: Twenty Metropolitan Regions*, Minneapolis: University of Minnesota Press.

Alcaly, R.E. and Memelstein, D. (1977) *The Financial Crisis of American Cities*, New York: Vintage.

Alexander, L.M. (1975) *The Northeastern United States*, London: Van Nostrand.

Allvine, F.C. and Tarpley, F.A. (1977) *The New State of the Economy*, Cambridge, Mass.: Winthrop.

Allaman, P.M. and Birch, D.L. (1975) *Components of Employment Change for Metropolitan and Rural Areas in the United States by Industry Group, 1970–2*, Cambridge, Mass.: Joint Center for Urban Studies of MIT and Harvard University, Working Paper No. 8.

Baker, O.E. (1926) "Agricultural regions of North America," *Economic Geography*, 2, 459–93.

Bell, D. (1973) *The Coming of Post-Industrial Society*, New York: Penguin.

Berry, B.J.L. (1963) *Commercial Structure and Commercial Blight*, Chicago: University of Chicago Department of Geography, Research Paper 85.

Berry, B.J.L. (1970) "The United States in the year 2000," *Transactions, Institute of British Geographers*, 51, 21–83.

Berry, B.J.L. (1973) *The Human Consequences of Urbanization*, New York: St Martin's Press.

Berry, B.J.L. (1973a) *Growth Centers in the American Urban System*, vols 1 and 2, Cambridge, Mass.: Ballinger.

Berry, B.J.L. (1975) "The decline of the ageing metropolis: cultural bases and social process," in Sternlieb, G. and Hughes, J.W., (eds) *Post-Industrial America: Metropolitan Decline and Inter-Regional Job Shifts*, New Brunswick, NJ: Center for Urban Policy Research, 175–86.

Berry, B.J.L. (1976) "The counterurbanization process: urban America since 1970," in Berry, B.J.L. (ed.) *Urbanization and Counterurbanization*, London: Sage, 17–30.

Berry, B.J.L. (1976a) *Chicago*, New York: Ballinger.

Berry, B.J.L. and Cohen, Y.S. (1975) *Spatial Components of Manufacturing Change, 1950–60*, Chicago: University of Chicago Department of Geography, Research Paper 172.

Berry, B.J.L. and Gillard, Q. (1976) *The Changing Shape of Metropolitan America: Commuting Patterns, Urban Fields and Decentralization Processes, 1960–70*, Cambridge, Mass.: Ballinger.

Bishop, C.E., Benson, R.S., Cafferty, S.J., Hinerfield, R.J., and Pace, F. (1980) *Urban America in the Eighties*, Washington: President's Commission for a national Agenda for the Eighties Report.

Bogue, D.J. (1959) *Population of the USA*, Chicago: Illinois Free Press.

Borchert, J.R. (1967) "American metropolitan evolution," *Geographical Review*, 57, 301–23.

Brown, M.A. (1980) "Attitudes and social categories: complementary explanations of innovation adoption," *Environment and Planning*, A, 12, 175–86.

Browning, C.E. and Gessler, W. (1979) "The sunbelt-snowbelt: a case of sloppy regionalizing," *Professional Geographer*, 31, 66–74.

Brunn, S.D. and Raitz, K. (1978) "Regional patterns of farm magazine publication," *Economic Geography*, 54, 277–90.

Brunn, S.D. and Wheeler, J.O. (1980) *The American Metropolitan System*, London: Arnold.

Brzezinski, Z. (1970) *Between Two Ages: America's Role in the Techneotronic Era*, New York: Viking Press.

Bureau of Census (1967) *200 Million Americans*, Washington: Department of Commerce.

Bureau of Census (1975) *Current Population Reports, Series P-25, No. 541*, Wahsington: Department of Commerce.

Burgess, E.W. (1925) "The growth of the city," in Park, R.E., Burgess, E.W., and McKenzie, R.D. (eds) *The City*, Chicago: University of Chicago Press, 47–62.

Bylinsky, G. (1974) "California's great breeding ground for industry," *Fortune*, 89, 128–35.

Calzonetti, F.J. (1980) "Energy and its effect on regional metropolitan growth in the United States," in Brunn, S.D. and Wheeler, J.O. (eds) *The American Metropolitan System*, London: Arnold, 181–200.

Catanese, A.J. (1979) "History and trends of urban planning," in Catanese, A.J. and Snyder, J.C. *Introduction to Urban Planning*, London: McGraw-Hill.

Caudill, H.M. (1962) *Night Comes to the Cumberlands*, Boston: Little, Brown & Co.

Clark, D. (1979) "The spatial impact of telecommunication," in Smith, R.C. (ed.) *Impacts of Telecommunication on Planning and Transport*, London: Departments of the Environment and Transport, Research Report 24. 85–128.

Claval, P., Forester, J., and Goldsmith, W.W. (1980) *Urban and Regional Planning in an Age of Austerity*, New York: Pergamon.

Cox, K.R. (1973) *Conflict, Power and Politics in the City: A Geographic View*, New York: McGraw-Hill.

Crevècoeur, J.H. St J. de (1782:1963) *Letters from an American Farmer* (1782); Signet edn, New York (1963), Letter III, "What is an American," 60–99.

Cumberland, J.H. (1971) *Regional Development Experiences and Prospects in the United States of America*, Paris: Mouton.

Dahrendorf, R. (1959) *Class and Class Conflict in an Industrial Society*, London: Routledge & Kegan Paul.

Daniels, P.W. (1975) *Office Location: An Urban and Regional Study*, London: Bell.

Dorel G. (1975) "La pénétration du grande capitalisme dans l'agriculture des Etats-Unis: le corporate farming," *Travaux de l'Institute de Geographie de Rheims*, vol. 21–2, 47–72.

Doxiadis, C.A. (1966) *Urban Renewal and the Future of the American City*, Chicago: Public Administration Service.

Doxiadis, C.A. (1969) *Ekistics: An attempt for a scientific approach to the problems of human settlements*, Paper presented to the Panel on Science and Technology of NASA.

Durand, L.B. (1964) "The major milksheds of the Northeastern quarter of the United States," *Economic Geography*, 40, 1–18.

Durant, T.J. and Knowlton, C.S. (1978) "Rural ethnic minorities: adaptive response to inequality," in Ford, T.R. (ed.) *Rural USA: Persistence and Change*, Ames, Iowa: Iowa State University Press, 145–67.

Estall, R.C. (1972) *A Modern Geography of the United States*, London: Pelican.

Estall, R.C. (1977) "Regional planning in the United States: an evaluation of experience under the 1965 Economic Development Act," *Town Planning Review*, 48, 341–64.

Estall, R.C. (1980) "The changing balance of the northern and southern regions of the United States," *Journal of American Studies*, 14, 315–86.

Estall, R.C. (1982) "Planning in Appalachia: an examination of the Appalachian regional development program and its implications for the future of the American Regional Planning Commissions," *Transactions, Institute of British Geographers*, New Series 7, 1, 35–58.

Evans, J.F. and Salcedo, R.N. (1974) *Communication in Agriculture: The American Farm Press*, Ames: Iowa State University Press.

Feldman, M.M. (1983) "Biotechnology and local economic growth: the American pattern," *Built Environment*, 9, 40–50.

Fortune (1956) "The 500 largest US industrial corporations," *Fortune*, 54 (Supplement).

Fortune (1976) "The Fortune Directory: the 500 largest US industrial corporations," *Fortune*, May, 316–37.

Galbraith, J.K. (1958) *The Affluent Society*, London: Hamish Hamilton.

Gans, H.J. (1962a) "Urbanism and suburbanism as ways of life," in Rose, A.M. (ed.) *Human Behaviour and Social Processes*, London: Routledge & Kegan Paul, 20–45.

Gans, H.J. (1962b) *The Urban Villagers*, New York: Free Press.

Gauthier, H.L. (1973) "The Appalachian Development Highway System: development for whom?" *Economic Geography*, 49, 103–8.

Geer, S. de (1927) "Delimitation of the North American manufacturing belt," *Geografiska Annaler*, 11, 247–58.

Golant, S.M. (1975) "Residential concentrations of the future elderly," *The Gerontologist*, 15, 16–23.

Golant, S.M. (1980) "Locational—environmental perspectives on old-age segregated areas in the United States," in Herbert, D.T. and Johnston, R.J. (eds) *Geography and the Urban Environment, vol. 3*, London: Wiley, 257–94.

Gottmann, J. (1961) *Megalopolis: The Urbanized Northeastern Seaboard of the United States*, New York: The Twentieth Century Fund.

Gregor, H. (1982) "Large-scale farming as a cultural dilemma in US rural development: the role of capital," *Geoforum*, 13, 1–10.

Hale, C.W. and Walters, J. (1974) "Appalachian regional development and distribution of highway benefits," *Growth and Change*, 5, 3–11.

Harris, C.D. (1954) "The market as a factor in the localization of industry in the United States," *Annals, Association of American Geographers*, 44, 315–48.

Hart, J.F. (1967) *The Southeastern United States*, London: Van Nostrand.

Hart, J.F. (1972) "The Middle West," in Hart, J.F. (ed.) *Regions of the United States*, London: Harper & Row, 258–82.

Hart, J.F. (1975) *The Look of the Land*, Englewood Cliffs, NJ: Prentice-Hall.

Hart, J.F. (1978) "Cropland concentrations in the south," *Annals, Association of American Geographers*, 68, 4, 505–17.

Hartshorne, R. (1936) "A new map of the manufacturing belt of North America," *Economic Geography*, 12, 45–53.

Heady, E.O. (1976) "The agriculture of the US," *Scientific American*, Sept. 1976, 106–27.

Heady, E.O., Haroldson, E.O., Mayer, L.V., and Tweeten, L.G. (1965) *Roots of the Farm Problem*, Ames, Iowa: Iowa State University Press.

Hill, R.C. (1977) "Fiscal collapse and political struggle in decaying central cities in the United States," in Tabb, W.K. and Sawers, L. (eds) *Marxism and the Metropolis: New Perspectives in Urban Political Economy*, Oxford: Oxford University Press, 213–40.

Horwood, E.M. and Boyce, R.R. (1959) *Studies of the Central Business District and Urban Freeway Development*, Seattle: University of Washington Press.

House, J.W. (1983) "Regional and area development," in House, J.W. (ed.) *United States and Public Policy*, Oxford: Oxford University Press, 34–79.

Janelle, D.G. (1969) "Spatial reorganization: a model and concept," *Annals, Association of American Geographers*, 59, 348–64.

Johnston, R.J. (1982) *The American Urban System*, London: Longman.

Johnson, J.H. and Brunn, S.D. (1980) "Spatial and behavioural aspects of the counterstream migration of blacks to the South," in Brunn, S.D. and Wheeler, J.O. (eds) *The American Metropolitan System*, London: Arnold, 59–76.

Johnston, M. and O'Rear, C. (1982) "Silicon Valley: cradle of the chip," *Geographical Magazine*, 162, 459–77.

Kahn, H. and Weiner, A.J. (1967) *The Year 2000*, New York: Macmillan.

Kelly, C.F. (1967) "Mechanical harvesting," *Scientific American*, August 1967, 50–9.

Kirwan, R. (1981) "The American experience," in Hall, P. (ed.) *The Inner City in Context*, London: Heinemann, 71–88.

Kivell, P.T. (1972) "Retailing in non-central locations," *Institute of Geographers*, Occasional Publication No. 1, 49–58.

Knox, P.L. (1982) "Residential structure, facility location and patterns of accessibility," in Cox, K.R. and Johnston, R.J. (eds) *Conflict, Politics and the Urban Scene*, London: Longman, 62–87.

Kollmorgan, W.M. and Jenks, G.F. (1958a) "Suitcase farming in Sully County, South Dakota," *Annals, Association of American Geographers*, 48, 27–40.

Kollmorgan, W.M. and Jenks, G.F. (1958b) "Sidewalk farming in Toole County, Montana, and Traill County, North Dakota," *Annals, Association of American Geographers*, 48, 209–31.

Kuehn, J.A. (1979) "Nonmetropolitan industrialisation and migration," in Lonsdale, R.E. and Seyler, H.L. (eds) *Nonmetropolitan Industrialisation*, London: Wiley, 137–48.

Levitan, S.A. (1964) *Federal Aid to Depressed Areas*, Baltimore: Johns Hopkins Press.

Lonsdale, R.E. (1979) "Background and issues," in Lonsdale, R.E. and Seyler, H.L. (eds) *Nonmetropolitan industrialisation*, London: Wiley, 3–9.

McClelland, D.C. (1961) *The Achieving Society*, New York: Van Nostrand.

McPheters, L.R. and Schlagenhauf, D.E. (1981) "Macroeconomic determinants of the flow of undocumented aliens in N. America," *Growth and Change*, 12, 2–8.

Malecki, E.J. (1980) "Science and technology in the American metropolitan system," in Brunn, S.D. and Wheeler, J.O. (eds) *The American Metropolitan System*, London: Arnold, 127–44.

Mandel, E. (1975) *Late Capitalism*, London: New Left Books.

Manners, G. (1974) "The office in metropolis: an opportunity for shaping metropolitan America," *Economic Geography*, 50, 93–110.

Meyer, J.W. (1983) "Social problems and policies," in House, J.W. (ed.) *United States Public Policy*, Oxford: Oxford University Press, 80–118.

Milk, R.G. (1972) "The new agriculture in the United States: a dissenter's view," *Land Economics*, 228–39.

Morrill, R.L. and Wohlenberg, E.H. (1971) *The Geography of Poverty in the United States*, London: McGraw-Hill.

Muller, P.O. (1973) "Trend surfaces of American agricultural patterns: a macro-Thunian analysis," *Economic Geography*, 49, 228–42.

Muller, P.O. (1980) "Suburbanisation in the 1970s: interpreting population, socio-economic and employment trends," in Brunn, S.D. and Wheeler, J.O. (eds) *The American Metropolitan System*, London: Arnold, 37–51.

Muller, P.O. (1981) *Contemporary Suburban America*, Englewood Cliffs, NJ: Prentice-Hall.

Munro, J.M. (1969) "Planning the Appalachian Development Highway System: some critical questions," *Land Economics*, 45, 149–61.

Murphy, R.E. (1972) *The Central Business District: A Study in Urban Geography*, London: Longman.

Murphy, R.E. and Vance, J.E. (1954a) "Delimiting the C.B.D.," *Economic Geography*, 30, 189–222.

Murphy, R.E. and Vance, J.E. (1954b) "A comparative study of nine central business districts," *Economic Grography*, 30, 301–36.

Murray, S. and Tweeten, L. (1981) "Culture, education, and economic progress on Federal Indian reservations," *Growth and Change*, 12, 10–16.

National Resources Planning Board (1937) *Our Cities: Their Role in the National Economy*, Washington, DC: National Resources Planning Board.

National Resources Planning Board (1939) *Urban Planning and Land Policies*, Washington, DC: National Resources Planning Board.

Norton, R.D. and Rees, J. (1979) "The product cycle and the spatial decentralization of American manufacturing," *Regional Studies*, 13, 141–51.

Odum, H.W. and Moore, H.E. (1938) *American Regionalism—A Cultural-Historical Approach to National Integration*, New York: H. Holt & Co.

OECD. (1980) *Regional Policies in the United States*, Paris: Organization for Economic Co-operation and Development.

Packard, V. (1961) *The Waste Makers*, London: Longman.

Palm, R. (1976) "The role of real estate agents as mediators in two American cities," *Geografiska Annaler*, 58B, 28–41.

PARC (1964) *Appalachia: A Report by the President's Appalachian Regional Commission*, Washington, DC.

Parsons, J.J. (1977) "Corporate farming in California," *Geographical Review*, 67, 354–7.

Perloff, H.S., Dunn, E.S., Lampard, E.E., and Muth, R.F. (1960) *Regions, Resources and Economic Growth*, Baltimore: Johns Hopkins Press.

Phillips, P.D. and Brunn, S.D. (1978) "Slow growth: a new epoch of American metropolitan evolution," *Geographical Review*, 68, 274–92.

Pred, A.R. (1965) "The concentration of high value-added manufacturing," *Economic Geography*, 41, 108–32.

Pred, A.R. (1977) *City Systems in Advanced Economies*, London: Hutchinson.

Prunty, M.C. (1951) "Recent quantitative changes in the cotton regions of the Southeastern States," *Economic Geography*, 27, 202–7.

Prunty, M.C. and Aiken, C.S. (1972) "The demise of the Piedmont cotton region," in Hart, J.F. (ed.) *Regions of the United States*, London: Harper & Row, 283–306.

Quante, W. (1975) *The Exodus of Corporate Headquarters from New York City*, New York: Praeger.

Rees, J. (1978) "Manufacturing headquarters in a post-industrial urban context," *Economic Geography*, 54, 337–54.

Rees, J. (1979) "Technological change and regional shifts in American manufacturing," *The Professional Geographer*, 31, 45–54.

Rees, J. and Weinstein, B.L. (1983) "Government policy and industrial location," in House, J.W. (ed.) *United States and Public Policy*, Oxford: Oxford University Press, 213–17.

Rostow, W.W. (1965) *The Stages of Economic Growth*, London: Cambridge University Press.

Rostow, W.W. (1977) "Regional change in the fifth Kondratieff upswing," in Perry, D.C. and Watkins, A.J. (eds) *The Rise of the Sunbelt Cities*, Beverly Hills, California: Sage.

Rust, E. (1975) *No Growth: Impacts on Metropolitan Areas*, Lexington, Mass.: Lexington Books.

Saxenian, A. (1983) "The genesis of Silicon Valley," *Built Environment*, 9, 7–17.

Semple, R.K. (1973) "Recent trends in the spatial concentration of corporate headquarters," *Economic Geography*, 49, 309–18.

Seninger, S.F. and Smeeding, T.M. (1981) "Poverty: a human resource-income maintenance perspective," in Hawley, A.H. and Mazie, S.M. (eds) *Nonmetropolitan America in Transition*, Chapel Hill, North Carolina: University of North Carolina Press, 382–436.

Servan-Schreiber, J.J. (1968) *The American Challenge*, London: Hamilton.

Seyler, H.L. and Lonsdale, R.E. (1979) "Implications for nonmetropolitan development policy," in Lonsdale, R.E. and Seyler, H.L. (eds) *Nonmetropolitan Industrialisation*, London: Wiley, 181–90.

Smith, D.M. (1973) *The Geography of Social Well-Being in the United States*, London: McGraw-Hill.

Smith, E. (1975) "Fragmented farms in the USA," *Annals, Association of American Geographers*, 65, 58–70.

Statistical Abstract of the United States (1981) Washington, DC: US Bureau of the Census.

Stephens, J.D. and Holly, B.P. (1980) "The changing patterns of industrial corporate control in metropolitan United States," in Brunn, S.D. and Wheeler, J.O. (eds) *The American Metropolitan System*, London: Arnold, 161–80.

Sternlieb, G. and Hughes, J.W. (1975) *Post-Industrial America: Metropolitan Decline and Inter-regional Job Shifts*, new Brunswick, NJ: Center for Urban Policy Research.

Sternlieb, G. and Hughes, J.W. (1978) "The new economic geography of America," in Sternlieb, G. and Hughes, J.W. (eds) *Revitalizing the Northeast: Prelude to an Agenda*, New Brunswick, NJ: Center for Urban Policy Research.

Suttles, G.D. (1975) "Community design: the search for participation in a metropolitan society," in Hawley, A.H. and Rock, V.P. (eds) *Metropolitan America in Contemporary Perspective*, New York: Halstead, 235–97.

Tabb, W.K. (1977) "The New York City fiscal crisis," in Tabb, W.K. and Sawers, L. (eds) *Marxism and the metropolis: New Perspectives in Urban Political Economy*, Oxford: Oxford University Press, 241–66.

Taeuber, C. and Taeuber, I. (1958) *The Changing Population of the United States*, London: Wiley.

Thistlethwaite, F. (1961) *Great Experiment: An Introduction to the History of the American People*, Cambridge: Cambridge University Press.

Thompson, W. (1975) "Economic processes and employment problems in declining metropolitan areas," in Sternlieb, G. and Hughes, J.W. (eds) *Post-industrial America: Metropolitan Decline and Inter-Regional Job Shifts*, New Brunswick, NJ: Center for Urban Policy Research, 187–98.

Thunen, J.H. Von (1826) *Der Isolierte Staat in Berziehung auf Landwirthshaft und Nationalökonomie*, Hamburg: Cotta.

Tienda, M. (1981) "The Mexican-American population," in Hawley, A.H. and

Mazie, S.M. (eds) *Nonmetropolitan America in Transition*, Chapel Hill, North Carolina: University of North Carolina Press, 502–48.

Turner, F.J. (1894) "The significance of the frontier in American history," *American Historical Association Annual Report for 1893*, Washington: American Historical Association, 199–227.

Ullman, E.L. (1954) "Amenities as a factor in regional growth," *Geographical Review*, 44, 119–32.

Vance, J.E. (1972) "California and the search for the ideal," in Hart, J.F. (1972) *Regions of the United States*, Washington: Association of American Geographers, 185–210.

Van Otten, G. (1980) "Changing spatial characteristics of Willamette Valley farms," *Professional Geographer*, 32, 63–71.

Vinje, D.L. (1977) "Income and labor participation on Indian reservations," *Growth and Change*, 8, 38–41.

Walsh, J. (1975) "US agribusiness and agricultural trends," *Science*, May 9, 1975, 531–4.

Warren, K. (1973) *The American Steel Industry 1850–1970*, Oxford: Oxford University Press.

Watson, J.W. (1979) *Social Geography of the United States*, London: Longman.

Watson, J.W. (1982) *The United States*, London: Longman.

Weinstein, B.L. and Firestine, R.E. (1978) *Regional Growth and Decline in the United States*, New York: Praeger.

Weaver, J.C. (1954) "Crop-combination regions in the Middle West," *Geographical Review*, 44, 175–200.

Webb, R.E. and Bruce, W.M. (1968) "Redesigning the tomato for mechanized production," *Science for Better Living: 1968 Yearbook of Agriculture*, Washington, DC: US Government Printing Office, 103–7.

Wheeler, J.O. and Muller, P.O. (1981) *Economic Geography*, London: Wiley.

Winsberg, M.D. (1980) "Concentration and specialization in United States agriculture," *Economic Geography*, 56, 183–9.

Wirth, L. (1938) "Urbanism as a way of life," *American Journal of Sociology*, 44, 1–24.

Wittwer, S.H. (1975) "Food production: technology and the resource base," *Science*, May 9, 579–84.

Index